The Empowered Grief Journey

The
EMPOWERED
GRIEF
Journey

23 Stories of Grief That
Carved a New Path Forward

GUIDED BY
CHRIS MAMONE

The Empowered Grief Journey™
Collected and edited by Chris Mamone
© 2025 The Empowered Grief Journey LLC
All rights reserved.

ISBNs:
Paperback (Amazon): 979-8-9937363-0-3
Paperback (IngramSpark): 979-8-9937363-1-0
eBook (IngramSpark): 979-8-9937363-2-7

The Empowered Grief Journey and the CADEN Framework™
are trademarks of Chris Mamone.
First Edition - 2025

Cover Design & Interior Layout by Kristina Mamone

Printed in the United States of America

For more resources visit:
www.empoweredgriefjourney.com

Connect with our community:
@empoweredgriefjourney

To my little lion,
Caden Petter Mamone.

Our time together was far too short,
yet your presence changed me forever.

The lessons you left behind continue
to shape the person I am becoming.

All the light in these pages
shines because of you.

CONTENTS

FOREWARD

However you've arrived at this moment, know this: you are exactly where you're meant to be. The universe has guided you to this book, and only you and your Creator know why. *The Empowered Grief Journey: 23 Stories of Grief That Carved A New Path Forward* is more than a collection of stories—it's a sanctuary of healing, love, and transformation.

Chris Mamone, the visionary behind this anthology, along with each contributing author, welcomes you with open hearts. We've come together to raise our voices in unity—to share our pain, our healing, and our hope. We understand grief intimately. We've lived it and survived it, and now we offer our stories to help light your path forward.

Chris's dream of fatherhood was shattered when his son Caden was stillborn on September 23, 2022. This book stands as a beautiful tribute to Caden's life and legacy. Chris and his wife Kristina have created The Empowered Grief Journey together to honour their son and help others find healing. Chris also hosts a podcast of the same name, offering a platform for others to share their stories of transformation, while supporting others in his role as a grief coach.

Through his pain, Chris has found purpose. He steps into this new path daily, guided by love and a higher calling. His work is helping countless others find their voice and begin their healing journey. Chris's loss and grief brought together every author in this book, and we stand as living proof that joy, love, and peace are possible after loss.

Each chapter in this book is a soul-baring journey. These are not just stories—they are lived experiences of people who have faced unimaginable loss and emerged with purpose. You'll find hope here. You'll find truth. And most importantly, you'll find connection.

I'm deeply honoured to write this foreword. Though I haven't met Chris in person, we've bonded through sharing our grief and healing journeys on each other's podcasts. When Chris told me he was creating this book in honour of his son Caden, I immediately understood the depth of his purpose. I saw not only his pain but the power of legacy—a legacy born from love, loss, and the desire to help other people heal.

This book is a testament to that legacy. It's a gift to a world that desperately needs compassion, understanding, and healing. Our hope is that by sharing our voices, we help shift the narrative around grief. Grief is not something to fear or suppress—it's something to feel, honour, and move through with love and kindness, both for ourselves and for others.

I said "yes" to writing this foreword without hesitation because

I've carried my own grief for decades. My journey began at birth. I was born with clubfeet to an unwed mother who gave me to her family to raise. My childhood was marked by abuse, violence, and addiction. By age five, I was already enduring physical and emotional abuse; by ten, I had survived trauma no child should face—including sexual abuse. At seventeen, I attempted suicide. It was in this darkest moment of my life that I first heard the voice of God say, "You're Not Finished Here Yet." I found strength and courage in those words.

I went on to endure a twenty-five-year abusive marriage, lost three pregnancies, and was failed by professionals I had desperately turned to for help. Grief consumed me. I mourned alone, even while caring for my grandmother until her death, which happened during my divorce. My world collapsed—my children abandoned me, and I lost the home I had lovingly created for my family. Yet, I found the strength to walk away and eventually met a man whose compassion saved me. We've now been married nineteen years.

Eight months into our marriage, I faced death in a head-on vehicle collision. Once again I heard God's voice. That moment marked a turning point. I mourned the loss of my physical health, my career, and my friends and family who did not know how to support me. Nine years into my recovery from catastrophic injuries, I wrote a book called *A Century of Secrets*. I co-authored several best-selling anthologies, as well as launching my podcast, *Powering Through Life*. In my quest to heal, I immersed myself in learning about the mind and its impact on our bodies, relationships, and lives. Today, I'm a certified NLP Results Coach, Master Practitioner of NLP, Time Line Therapy®, Hypnotherapy, and Breakthrough Profile Evaluator.

Through this journey, I discovered how deeply grief had embedded itself in my body, mind and soul—manifesting itself as

DIS-EASE, (disease). Grief was consuming me. Now, I understand grief not just emotionally but also physically and spiritually. I've learned to process it, and I continue to heal everyday—just as every author in this book has done. That is our wish for you. To find peace, healing, and grace.

Born from this healing journey, my personal affirmation is one I say out loud to myself every day:

> *"I am a radiant force of healing and transformation. My past has shaped my power, not my limits. I rise with clarity, speak with purpose, lead with compassion. I am here to light the path for others, turning pain into purpose and silence into strength."*

Grief touches every life—through the loss of loved ones, relationships, careers, health, or identity. It is a natural response to loss, and it deserves to be honoured. The purpose of this book is to share stories of survival and transformation. And to remind you that you are not alone!

Before you begin reading, take a deep breath, relax and open your heart and mind. We suggest reading one story at a time. This will allow you space and time to reflect while absorbing each author's journey. Write down your thoughts in a journal. Give yourself permission to feel, absorb our words and return to this healing book as many times as you need. If a particular story resonates with you, reach out to the author. Let their strength and bravery inspire your own transformation.

Together, we are building a community—a space of support, understanding, and healing. We've faced our grief, walked through the trauma, and now stand united in love and light. Within these pages, you'll find stories written with profound understanding of how grief affects the human spirit and soul.

Let us walk with you through your Empowered Grief Journey. Know that you are not alone. Each author has written with truth, love, and a commitment toward their healing.

Grief is not the end—it's the beginning of something new, something sacred. This book is a legacy to Caden Petter Mamone. May his life remind us all that death is not the end—it is a teacher, a healer, and a stepping-stone to transformation.

From grief, we are reborn.

We, the survivors and thrivers of grief, understand your desire to heal. We are traveling this journey with you. Place your hand on your heart and feel the healing love being sent to you.

"When we sit in silence and truly listen to the lessons and meanings of the gifts we receive through this experience, life will begin again—with purpose, passion, and healing."

Teresa Syms
Ontario, Canada
October, 2025

PREFACE

I created *The Empowered Grief Journey: 23 Stories of Grief That Carved A New Path Forward* to honor my son Caden who was stillborn on September 23rd, 2022, one day before he was supposed to be born. Our time together was heartbreakingly short, yet his presence continues to shape my life in profound ways. This book is part of the legacy I am creating to honor his memory. Through these pages, I hope to show you how grief can hold a deeper and more empowering impact in our lives than modern western societies have conditioned us to believe.

The idea for this anthology grew out of my six-month experience creating *The Empowered Grief Journey*™ podcast. I had been battling depression after losing Caden and longed for a way to share his story. A friend introduced me to podcasting, assuring me it would be both healing and rewarding. At first, I was nervous to be interviewed, let alone speak publicly about my grief. But as I connected with podcast hosts through Facebook groups, I began sharing Caden's story on shows about grief, trauma, self-improvement, and empowerment, and I found my voice in the process.

After several guest appearances, other hosts encouraged me to start my own show, and *The Empowered Grief Journey*™ podcast was born. I posted invitations for guests who had powerful grief stories and healing journeys to share. From the beginning, I was quickly flooded with responses—sometimes thirty to fifty comments on a single post. My calendar filled up so quickly that I was recording nearly ten episodes a week.

During my conversations with guests, I began to see a painful truth: Grief is deeply misunderstood across the world. No matter where my guests were from, they told similar stories. Support from friends, family, and colleagues would be there for a short time and then fade away. The grief-stricken guests would commonly hear phrases like, "You need to let go" or "It's time to move on." The message from the outside world was clear: Grief had an expiration date.

My guests' stories proved the opposite. Many were carrying their grief for years or decades after their loss, but not in a way that kept them stuck. For some, grief became a guide that reshaped their lives. They changed careers, moved to new places, wrote books, became coaches, and found powerful ways to help others through empathetic and compassionate work. I began to realize that grief and healing are not linear journeys. Instead, grief leads us towards a deeply personal transformation that involves shedding an old version of yourself and stepping into who you are becoming.

One guest summed it up perfectly when they told me, "Grief

chose you, and you chose grief." Looking back on my life, I began to realize that grief had been walking alongside me for many years. Most recently, I left my hometown of Tacoma, Washington, in 2018 and moved across the country to Concord, New Hampshire, leaving behind my mother, grandmother, and terminally ill grandfather. I returned home in August of 2020, just in time to hold my grandfather as he took his last breath. In 2022, I lost my job, and three months later, Caden.

Losing Caden was the pivotal moment when my entire world collapsed. My grief journey felt like pulling the tower card from a tarot deck—a sudden destruction of everything I thought was stable, forcing me to rebuild from the ground up. Grief dismantled my connections with people around me, jobs, and beliefs, stripping away what no longer served me. Yet in the rubble, I chose empowerment. I began to see that grief was shaping who I was becoming, calling me to shed the outdated beliefs that kept me from living with true meaning and purpose. Shortly after his passing, I told my wife, "Everything great that comes next in our life starts with Caden."

After recording nearly one hundred episodes on my podcast and having deeply powerful conversations centered around grief and healing, I realized that something much bigger than me was taking shape. Several guests had encouraged me to write a book, and the idea of putting together an anthology occurred to me. When I invited my most memorable podcast guests to contribute, they all said yes without hesitation.

Caden was born on September 23rd, 2022, and ever since he passed, I see the number 23 everywhere. In honor of his memory, this anthology holds 23 chapters; 23 stories of grief that carved a new path forward. This book was created in the silence that followed the deepest loss of my life. In the time since losing Caden, I found myself searching not just for answers, but for other voices that understood the pain of grief and loss that I couldn't put into words. Looking back, I wish there had been a collection of voices like those found in this anthology when grief first upended my life.

Chris Mamone
Gig Harbor, Washington, USA
November, 2025

INTRODUCTION

In today's world, grief is often hidden, silenced, and misunderstood. We're taught to quiet our pain, suppress our emotions, and "move on" in ways that betray the needs of our mind, body, and spirit. These outdated approaches leave countless people feeling unseen, unheard, and misunderstood for grieving in ways that are natural and deeply personal to their grief experience. *The Empowered Grief Journey*™ was created to transform how we see and experience grief.

Grief is not a shadow to suppress or a burden to escape. It's a living part of you that transforms as you begin your healing journey—not something to outgrow, abandon, or forget. It gives rise to a profound process of personal growth that moves us beyond who we were in our life before loss, and calls us to step into who we are becoming. Grief can be a powerful teacher that fosters courage, reveals truth, and awakens our souls to the depth of our humanity.

Grief is universal and uniquely expressed. The chapters you're about to read are a collection of grief stories and healing journeys from people around the world. These stories show that grief does not discriminate and that healing takes many forms across various cultures, perspectives, and individual voices. Through these collective voices, we can navigate grief with courage and compassion. Together, these stories reveal that grief is not the end of our story but the beginning of a new chapter in our lives—one that invites **C**ourage, **A**cceptance, **D**eep Healing, **E**mpowerment, and **N**ew Beginnings (**CADEN**).

Within the rawness of our grief dwell
hidden gifts, lessons, and blessings that
guide us toward healing and renewal.

Each story in this anthology was written by a different author, sharing a unique grief and healing journey in a raw, vulnerable, and authentic voice. You'll discover how each author found the unexpected gifts, lessons, and blessings within their pain that are guiding them toward who they are becoming today. Themes include the loss of a child, surviving abuse, and the sudden passing of a loved one. Together, these stories remind us that grief arises in many forms and touches every corner of life. If a story resonates deeply, you can connect with the author through their bio and media links at the end of each chapter.

This anthology offers a safe place—free of judgment and ex-pectations—where you can meet yourself exactly where you are in your grief journey. These pages do not shy away from the emotional intensity of loss. They illuminate the moments when you discover your resilience, the quiet practice of carrying grief forward, allowing it to transform you, and walking beside it as you grow into who you are becoming.

Grief is like the ocean: some days the waves crash so hard
they threaten to pull you under; other days the waters
are calm enough to let you breathe. Within this ebb and
flow lives the courage, compassion, patience, and
understanding that shapes resilience.

What you read may stir something deep within you—and that's okay. Let these emotions be messengers: meet them with compassion and allow them to guide you toward the next small step on your healing path. These stories may help you discover your own Empowered Grief Journey.

Your grief story and healing journey are uniquely yours. They don't have to make sense to anyone else. You don't have to heal on anyone's timeline or measure your grief against that of other people. You don't have to change how you grieve. You're walking this journey exactly as you need to. So let's walk it together—one story at a time.

You are seen.
You are heard.
You are understood.
You are not broken.
You do not need to be fixed.

You may be moving through grief or feeling stuck. You might feel lost, overwhelmed, numb, curious, or even quietly hopeful. All of it is valid. Give yourself permission to grieve and heal in your own way. Move through these chapters at your own pace, skip, pause, and return when you're ready. Highlight what resonates with you and journal about what thoughts arise so you can connect with your grief, get in touch with your own wisdom, and explore a way forward that feels true to you.

Consider this book a compass and the voices within it your companions on the road ahead. Here, you are invited to honor your path, embrace your emotions, and find strength in your own time. Emotional healing is a journey, not a destination. One step at a time, one page at a time, you will find your way forward.

As you move through these stories, may you find the **Courage** to face your pain, the **Acceptance** to meet it with compassion, the **Depth** to heal what has been hidden, the **Empowerment** to reclaim your voice, and the **New Beginnings** that await beyond your grief.

This is your Empowered Grief Journey—a path of transformation, connection, and renewal. You are not walking alone. These pages are here to remind you that within your grief lives the same light that guides every story in this book: the light of healing, hope, and rebirth.

Welcome to the Empowered Grief Journey.

1

CADEN'S COURAGE
THE STRENGTH TO BEGIN AGAIN

Chris Mamone

I will never forget the night my wife and I raced to the triage center at the hospital. Our minds were filled with anxiety, desperately clinging to hope and trying not to fear the worst. It felt like seconds after the nurse began the ultrasound that we heard the words no parent wants to hear, "There's no heartbeat." What was supposed to be one of the happiest and most joyful moments of my life quickly became the hardest, most unimaginable loss.

2022 was the most difficult year of my life. I faced relentless hardship and challenges financially and emotionally. As the new year began, I was focused on starting my new job at a local bank, helping my wife grow her pottery business, and setting up my woodshop in our garage. It was time to start creating the inspiring life we had always talked about. In January, as I started a rough day at work, my wife came into my office and told me she was pregnant. I jumped out of my office chair and lifted her off the ground with a bear hug and shared my passionate excitement; after six years of trying to conceive, I was going to be a father!

Becoming a father for the first time is like stepping into the unknown. I learned quickly to trust the process and be present every step of the way. I went with my wife to every check-in with our midwife and to every ultrasound appointment. I listened. I asked questions. There were so many moments that brought joy and excitement to me. I recorded Caden's heartbeat at every appointment. I felt his little hand run across mine as I held my wife's belly. He would move around in all sorts of different positions every day. He was full of life and constantly moving.

As we approached our due date, we spent time fixing up our house and creating a nursery for Caden upstairs next to our bedroom. We lived in a small house in the woods of New Hampshire on a five-acre property surrounded by woods and tall trees. We would spend time having breakfast outside in the mornings listening and watching the birds, deer, and other wildlife wander around our property. We would sit outside at night on our patio having little bonfires and watching the sun go down behind the trees to expose the clear night sky full of stars and a moon so bright it would light up the yard like daytime. Our home in the woods was our quiet place of calm away from the world.

One afternoon, I was cutting and stacking firewood in preparation for the harsh winters we experienced living in New England. My wife came out and told me she was concerned because she had noticed Caden's movements had stopped. While everything had been going smoothly during our pregnancy, we decided to have our midwife come by the house and check on Caden to see if there was any reason for concern. What happened next was a blurred rushing drive to the triage center at the hospital.

That moment in the emergency room felt like a nightmare that I wished I could wake up from. I was holding my wife's hand, staring at a monitor watching the nurse point to where a heart should have been beating and explaining that there was no heartbeat. I watched my wife go into shock, screaming at the nurses that this couldn't be happening, it wasn't real. My mind went numb in the middle of the chaos. I couldn't understand how a baby that was so active and full of life suddenly had passed away. How could a pregnancy with no issues suddenly become every parent's worst nightmare? Everything inside me was screaming that there had to be something we could do, some way to fix this. *This can't be.* As I shifted through a range of emotions from being completely numb to intense waves of shock and panic, I was in utter disbelief. In the previous nine months, I had managed to lose my job, get emotionally and verbally abused by my in-laws, and now I lost my only child. Caden was the one part of my life that gave me hope and a reason to keep going in life, despite all of the challenges I had faced that year. Now he was taken away from me, too. Caden had passed one day before we were supposed to bring him into the world.

I got up the next morning after a sleep-deprived restless night full of anxiety and shock. Before we headed back to the hospital, I remember telling my wife, "We are going to meet our son." On September 23, 2022, at 7:58 p.m., Caden Petter Mamone was born weighing 7 pounds, 12 ounces. Once I held him, I didn't want to let go. He had the cutest little button nose and tiny fingers that wrapped around mine. Caden stole the hearts of our midwife and the nurses in the delivery room that evening. They all shared how cute and sweet his little face was. Later that night, the nurses let us know that they invited a local photographer to come take pictures of us as a family the next day.

Saying goodbye to Caden was the hardest moment of my life. I had so little time with him, and would have given up everything to have more time with him. I remember holding him, talking to him, telling him how much I loved him. I am so grateful to our nurse, Chandler, who was there for us from the moment we found out his heart had stopped to the moment we had to go home without him. She held Caden in a rocking chair as we left the hospital, comforting him with love. In less than 48 hours, what was supposed to be a happy new beginning to our family now became a journey into the deepest grief of unimaginable loss.

The evening we drove home from the hospital was a mixture of raw numbness and intense anger burning inside me. As I sat at the first traffic light on our drive home, my mind was racing. The feeling of going back to reality and all the pressures we faced before losing Caden had become unbearable. A powerful thought of clarity came forward in the stillness and quiet of that moment. I couldn't go back to my old life. It simply wasn't going to work. It was finally time to shed every aspect of my life that no longer served me. It was time for a massive change. It was time to create a new life from scratch.

The first year after losing Caden was filled with relentless waves of grief and intense emotions. I was consumed by anger, numbness, and a crushing feeling of depression that felt like it would never end. It was the start of a new chapter in my life, a transformational rebirth filled with a series of subtle, painful shifts that destroyed aspects of my life that were no longer serving me. There were days where I felt "normal," while other days were a struggle to leave the house.

On the 23rd of every month, I'd wake up filled with anger. I never planned it, never expected it, but my grief knew the date. It took me some time to realize that those days marked a visceral reminder that Caden wasn't here with me. I was lost inside my own emotions, unsure of how to make sense of what I was feeling or how to move forward. I was angry that the life I had planned for was taken away from us in an instant. A potent reminder of what we had lost stood against the wall in our little upstairs nursery—an empty crib in which our baby boy would never fall asleep nor wake up. I was left standing in the dark abyss of grief trying to figure out what the purpose of my life would be going forward.

A couple months after Caden had passed, I decided to build a box for his ashes. As I began gluing the pieces of wood together, the wood refused to come together in the way I needed it to. My grief quickly surged into frustration and disappointment. I threw the box on the ground and tried to smash it with my foot, only the box didn't break. My heel did. I ended up walking on crutches for six weeks and was now carrying the weight of my grief physically and emotionally. I will never forget crawling up the basement stairs that day, crying, swearing, and hurting in every way. In the middle of this breakdown, I had a breakthrough. My anger was the part of me that loved me the most. It was my love for Caden with nowhere to go. I was being called to listen to my emotions instead of trying to suppress them. They were messengers trying to communicate what grief was trying to show me.

Another wave of grief surged through me one day while I was hobbling down our driveway to get the mail. A powerful windstorm had swept through our area during the first year we lived in our home. I remember after the storm noticing that a tree had snapped across the street from our mailbox. Two of the branches had been thrown high into the branches of another tree, wedging themselves in a way that formed the shape of a cross, like you would see in church. That cross became a place where I would talk to God, ask for answers, and sit with my grief.

My emotions overtook me as I spoke to God. I picked up rocks and hurled them at the cross, screaming and cursing at God for allowing Caden to be taken from me. I was mad at Him for allowing this to happen. The rage gave way to tears as I collapsed into surrender. I told God I was done trying to control or force the direction of my life. I asked him to guide me on this new path going forward, transforming my spiritual journey from solitude into companionship.

September 23rd, Caden's birthday, is the hardest and most special day of the year for me. It's a day filled with emotion, memories, and love for my little boy. I always find myself wondering what our lives would be like if he were still here. In honor of his memory, my wife and I created traditions that keep his spirit alive. Before Caden was born, my wife gifted all of us matching lion shirts. The lion became representative of Caden, a symbol of strength and courage. Every year on his birthday we wear our lion shirts with pride and remembrance.

We also bake him a homemade three-tier safari cake with chocolate and vanilla layers, frosted in white and green. It's decorated with lion family figurines, little trees, and sparkler candles that light up the room with his spirit. We look through photos from the day he was born and share our stories of grief and love from the moment we met our little man. September 23rd has become our day to celebrate all things Caden. Honoring him in this way has helped us heal and continue carrying him forward in the lives we're building after his loss.

My grief with Caden became my greatest teacher, reshaping every part of my life. I learned that grief is a personal transformation journey that takes away everything in your life that no longer fits and challenges you to rebuild yourself by integrating the depth of your loss. There is no "moving on" or "getting over it." There is only moving forward and through your grief.

One of the hardest lessons I had to learn in my healing journey after losing Caden was finding acceptance. It was not comforting or easy, and it didn't make me feel better as I began to heal from losing him. I discovered that acceptance was the ability to surrender to the present moment and let go of the fight against reality. It took me two years to release my resistance to reality and become the observer of my life rather than trying to fix it. This shift changed everything for my healing journey. Acceptance showed me that grief is life in a new form. It cracks you open, reshapes you, and calls you to question who you're becoming. There's no map, no timeline, and no going back to your old life. There is only a new version of you, rising from the ashes with deeper empathy, truth, and strength.

As I stepped into this new version of myself, I realized that my grief and healing are not destinations with an end but a deeply personal journey which follows a path that is unpredictable and often circular. Some days, I feel grounded and full of hope. Other days, I feel like I'm starting from scratch. Healing moves in waves, not along milestones.

I was surprised in my healing journey to discover that my anger wasn't the enemy; it was my fiercest protector. My anger was the part of me that loved me the most. It would rise up to defend the areas of my heart that were broken from the grief of losing Caden. Beneath my anger was the raw and unfiltered love for my son. Grief and anger are twins in disguise, both born from the same place that says, "This loss matters, my pain is real, and my love is powerful." My anger uncovered the grief I was still carrying, the parts of me that hadn't yet been allowed to fully feel the weight of losing Caden. Anger was trying to communicate a truth that I couldn't say out loud. Caden mattered more to me than words could describe.

As I continued to heal and listen to my anger, I learned that my emotions were not problems to be solved or to be controlled and suppressed. My emotions were messengers that carried wisdom to help guide me along my healing journey. They drew attention to unhealed parts of myself that were crying for attention to be seen, heard, and understood. I began to hold space for my emotions without shame or judgment. I stopped trying to ignore my emotions or trying to control their intensity and began to start healing from my grief.

Three years later, as I write this, I'm not in a place of "completion" but a place of presence. I still grieve. I still talk to Caden and cry on his birthday. But I have also created a deep meaning and purpose around his life. I became empowered to build a life where his memory inspires the work I do every day. I've stepped into a purpose that would never have unfolded had he not come into my life the way he did. My grief is the foundation of everything I am moving forward into in my life.

Today, I am the founder of *The Empowered Grief Journey*™, a coaching and podcast platform that helps individuals move from a place of pain to empowerment through their grief. I coach people around the world who are navigating grief, loss, and trauma to rediscover their self-acceptance and personal power to create an inspiring future grounded in healing, truth, and purpose. I have recorded over 100 episodes on my podcast where guests share real conversations, powerful stories, and guiding insights to help others discover that even in the depths of loss, grief can become a pathway to empowerment in their lives.

The experience of losing Caden became the most profound transformation of my life. Grief broke me open, pulling me into deeper purpose, truth, and healing. My invitation to you is this: step into your own Empowered Grief Journey. Discover the quiet strength that acceptance brings, and embrace healing not as a destination, but as a lifelong unfolding. Grief is like the ocean—sometimes calm, sometimes stormy, always shifting. The only way forward is through the waves, never around them. Grief isn't the end of your story but a new beginning, one written with courage and unshakable strength. Step forward boldly, for every wave carries you closer to who you were always meant to become.

CHRIS MAMONE

Chris Mamone is an Acceptance Coach and the Founder of *The Empowered Grief Journey*™, a coaching and podcast platform that helps individuals move from pain to empowerment through their grief. He supports those navigating grief, loss, and trauma to rediscover self-acceptance and step into their personal power by creating inspiring futures grounded in healing, truth, and purpose.

CONNECT WITH CHRIS HERE

www.empoweredgriefjourney.com/chris

https://empoweredgriefjourney.podbean.com

Scan to learn more about Chris

2

CADEN'S COURAGE
FINDING MY VOICE

Kristina DeFazio-Mamone

After struggling with infertility for over six years, my husband Chris and I started 2022 with a miracle; we were finally pregnant! We were so happy, grateful, and honestly in disbelief that this was actually happening. Our dream of having a family was finally coming true.

Nine months later, fear struck when I went into early labor and noticed our baby wasn't moving. We raced to the hospital, clinging to hope even as dread filled the space. The nurse placed the ultrasound wand on my belly, and we held our breath. Then she said the words no parent should ever hear…

"There's no heartbeat."

I fell apart in a way that shattered every part of me—screaming, shaking, cursing at the universe, at anyone who could hear me. I kept yelling, "I am not accepting this! I am not ok!" The truth was too big and too cruel to accept. We had spent nine months going to every appointment, listening to his heartbeat, feeling every kick, and getting ready for his arrival—counting down the days until we'd finally get to meet our little boy. All of that excitement and anticipation collapsed in an instant. Six long years of waiting for the chance to have a family—*gone*. I felt myself go empty inside. I didn't know how to exist anymore, how to keep breathing in a world where my son was gone.

We were sent home that night, and at the time I didn't understand why. *Cut me open, get him out now!* Why weren't they doing something? In that moment, I clung to irrational hope, convinced there had to be a way to save him. I refused to accept he was gone and that there was nothing they could do.

We didn't sleep at all that night. I laid there in the dark, still pregnant, my son's lifeless body still inside me. Chris held me close as I kept shaking my head, whispering, *"No...this can't be real."* It felt like a nightmare—one I knew I would never wake up from. There was no escape—no moment where I would get him back. How could this be happening?

That night, I decided I wanted a C-section. I wanted it to be "over with." I thought if it happened fast enough, maybe it would hurt less. The idea of going through labor felt unbearable—I was already completely broken. But the truth was, I was scared. Scared to meet my son and fall in love with him. Scared to hold him, knowing I had to let him go. I wasn't avoiding the pain of labor, I was avoiding the heartbreak. How was I supposed to survive this?

When we returned to the hospital the next morning, I began to understand why they had sent us home. They understood how devastating this was and didn't want us making decisions from our fragile state of shock. After the nurses calmly and compassionately explained our options, something inside me shifted. I changed my mind about the delivery.

This will forever be one of the best decisions I ever made. Those eight hours of labor and delivery became memories of pain, strength, courage and love that Chris and I will cherish forever. We faced it together. Chris held me up through every single contraction—which was intense and relentless because of the pitocin I was given to speed up labor. I also stubbornly waited until I was ten centimeters and ready to push to get an epidural. And then the physical pain ended, and I held him in my arms.

Caden Petter Mamone.

Our beautiful little boy. I couldn't stop looking at him—touching his soft cheeks, kissing his little lips, taking in every detail of his face. I wanted to memorize him, to hold onto every second. I had been so afraid to face this moment, afraid of how deeply I would love him. But as I held him, I stopped fighting what was already true. And in that quiet surrender, I fell in love with my son.

Losing Caden was the deepest, most devastating heartbreak I have ever known, but it wasn't the only loss I was carrying. At the same time, a different kind of pain was unfolding—one that had been there long before I ever held my son.

Grieving the Family I Never Had

We often endure far more than we should from the people we love. But becoming a mother shifted everything for me. Suddenly, I wasn't just protecting myself—I was protecting the little life growing inside of me. From the moment I learned I was pregnant, something changed within me. I found my voice, and with it, the courage to finally speak my truth.

I knew that if I wanted to create a safe and healthy environment for my child, something had to change. I could see the unhealthy dynamics in my family, and I could no longer pretend they didn't exist. I felt called to face them. So I began having honest conversations with my mother, hoping she might meet me with understanding, compassion, and support.

Unfortunately…she did not.

My pregnancy brought out the worst in my mom. Instead of celebrating this miracle with us by respecting and supporting our choices, she created chaos around it. She tried to control every detail of our pregnancy, inserting herself into decisions that were never hers to make. Every conversation felt like a battle—she was argumentative and strategically undermining me at every turn.

I was constantly fighting to be seen, heard, understood and respected. Instead, my feelings were dismissed. Somehow everything became my fault. There was never any accountability from her, never a pause to consider the harm she was causing me. I spent so much of my pregnancy defending myself—explaining, clarifying, justifying—desperately trying to be understood. And it wasn't just her. I fought to be heard by my dad, sister, and brother too. They were unable to recognize that this moment was about us—Chris and I growing our family. They treated our pregnancy as if it belonged to them.

As the dysfunction became more evident, slowly and painfully, I began to see the truth. I found myself replaying conversations, questioning my reactions, and trying to understand why my mother left me feeling emotionally drained. No matter how much I grew, she never acknowledged the woman I was becoming. She didn't see the strength I was building, the independence I was claiming, or the life I was working so hard to create. She didn't treat me as her adult daughter with a voice of my own. Instead she tried to keep me small, in the role that served her needs best. To her, I was never my own person—just an extension of herself, someone expected to comply, rather than someone she respected and valued.

Eventually, the pattern became undeniable. The behavior that had shaped so much of my life wasn't normal. It had a name. My mother was a narcissist.

Narcissistic abuse is often dismissed because outsiders can't see it. No bruises, no marks, no visible wounds—it's psychological abuse that remains unseen from everyone but yourself. It shows up as manipulation, gaslighting, and subtle tactics meant to chip away at your confidence and sense of reality.

It traps you in a fog of confusion. You begin to second-guess your reactions, your memories, even your own truth because your feelings are minimized, your experiences are denied, and your boundaries are ignored. You find yourself wondering if you're "too sensitive" or "too emotional", because that's exactly what they want you to believe. They tear you down and make you feel like you have no value.

When you finally react to the mistreatment—when you express hurt, anger, or confusion—they flip the narrative. The narcissist will cast themselves as the victim and present you as the problem, carefully rearranging the story so others see them as innocent and you as irrational. That's the cycle and cruelty of narcissistic abuse.

This is what I experienced while I was pregnant with Caden. I was abused, bullied, and emotionally beaten down by my own family while I was doing the most beautiful and sacred thing a woman can do—growing life.

From the moment I found out I was pregnant, I felt a deep peace settle inside me. After six years of infertility, Chris and I felt nothing but blessed. We didn't have room for fear. We weren't obsessing, over-planning, or trying to control every detail. We were taking it one day at a time and savoring every moment in our way. But that calmness didn't sit well with my family. Narcissists do not like calm, they thrive on chaos.

Almost immediately, my mom and sister began projecting their own fears and anxieties onto me. They made every attempt to pull me into that stress—to match their panic, their urgency, their need to control. And when I didn't react how they wanted, they became frustrated and irritated. Often lashing out at me, telling me the pregnancy wasn't going the way they wanted and accusing me of being overly emotional when I would defend myself against their attacks.

I tried to explain how Chris and I wanted to approach this pregnancy—with peace and presence—but they didn't respect that. They had already created rigid expectations in their minds about how everything "should" go, and when reality didn't match the story they had constructed, they blamed me. Their disappointment became my responsibility. Their reactions became my burden. I began to see how their behavior centered around their own needs, not mine. My pregnancy became something they tried to manage and control, rather than something they supported me through. Their emotions took priority over my experience.

At twenty weeks we went in for our ultrasound—we would finally find out if we were having a boy or a girl. I already knew. From the beginning, I felt it. I can't explain how, but I just did. Maybe that's what people mean when they talk about a mother's intuition.

After the appointment, we were glowing with excitement. We

held that moment close, just the two of us, savoring the joy of finally being able to say it out loud: we were having a boy!

Because of the chaos and stress my mom had already created, Chris and I decided it was time for stronger boundaries. We decided to keep this exciting news to ourselves for a little while as we decided how we wanted to share it. So when my mom called to ask how the appointment went, I told her everything was perfect: baby was healthy, and so was I. Then she asked the question I knew was coming.

"What's the sex?"

I calmly said, "We're going to wait a little before sharing that."

She did not like that. She didn't respect our decision. She didn't accept the boundary—narcissists dislike boundaries of any kind. Instead, she immediately tried to get around it.

She'd say things like, "So... is *she* moving a lot?"

Her tone was teasing, but the intention was clear—to trick me into slipping up. To get the information she believed she was entitled to. After the call, I sent a group text to my whole family with the ultrasound photos. They responded with excitement, and then my mom wrote:

"And the sex is?" She was undermining me, again.

Trying to avoid a fight, I responded lightly: something like, "Everyone can make their guesses, but we're not telling yet." Playfully followed with a winky face emoji.

That was met with confusion, irritation, and pressure. They wanted the information on their terms, and they were annoyed that I wasn't giving it to them. That's when I started to see it clearly: the unhealthy enmeshment my mother had created in our family. Later, I'd learn this is common in narcissistic family systems—lack of boundaries, oversharing, punishing independence, and suppressing individuality. Your identity, emotions, and decisions don't belong to you, they belong to the family. You are just a pawn in the game they are playing.

In her mind, my baby was **her** baby. She even said those exact words to me, "How's *my* baby doing?"

Eventually I tried to talk to my mom, hoping—naively—that she would acknowledge how disrespectful she had been. Instead, it exploded into another fight. She deflected everything, refusing to acknowledge even the smallest part of her behavior.

"That's not what happened," she'd say. "You're overreacting." My feelings were dismissed, my words dissected, and the blame was shifted entirely onto me.

Then she pulled the rest of my family into it. I felt physically sick one day when she said, "There are four of us and only one of you—so who do you think is wrong?" As if my feelings could be outvoted. This is called triangulation, one of the most common tactics in narcissistic abuse, used to isolate and shame the person speaking up. I realized truth didn't matter in this family—only obedience and control. This chaos was all happening because I was no longer willing to play her game.

For so long, I thought these behaviors were just "family quirks"—the annoying traits you learn to tolerate, the things you excuse because you're taught to love them *anyway*. I convinced myself this was normal. But these weren't quirks. This was not normal. This was harmful.

I was hurt. I was disappointed. I felt abandoned by the people who were supposed to protect me—especially now, as I was carrying my child, when I needed gentleness most. I had spent years convincing myself that my family was loving and supportive. Denying my own pain and unmet needs for too long. I found myself grieving something I didn't even know I had been missing my whole life: the family I never actually had, the love I never received.

I cried for the mother who was never able to love me.

I cried for the father who never protected me.

I cried for the siblings who chose comfort instead of truth.

I cried for the little girl inside me who didn't receive the emotional support she desperately needed.

I grieved every version of myself who stayed loyal to people who were hurting me.

I deserved love. I deserved support. I deserved safety.

Giving myself space to feel all of these emotions and to acknowledge this grief, was the first real step in healing wounds I had been carrying since childhood.

My Greatest Gift

A few months after Caden died, my mom called. I was drowning in grief—barely sleeping, barely functioning, shattered by the trauma of what we were surviving. I didn't have the capacity for her chaos, her drama, or her insensitive comments. So I didn't answer her multiple calls.

She left a voicemail, irritation unmistakable in her tone: "Hey Krissy, I was just calling to see how you're feeling. I've called you three times now and you haven't called me back. Do we need to *talk?*"

Even after losing my son, she couldn't offer a single word of real compassion. No softness, no empathy, no unconditional love. She still hadn't acknowledged how she treated me during the pregnancy—no apology, no ownership. She wasn't calling to see how I was feeling; she was calling because I wasn't meeting her expectations. Once again, her feelings mattered more than my loss. Even in my deepest grief, she was trying to pull me back into her cycle of control, abuse, and cruelty.

I didn't want to lose my family. I had fought so hard my entire life to preserve it. But something inside me finally understood: it was never my job to work so hard for love and respect that should have come effortlessly. I was finally accepting them for who they are—and who they are unable to be for me.

I haven't spoken to my family in three years. It remains one of the best decisions I've ever made—for my life, my marriage, and my emotional well-being. In the space they left behind, I found clarity. I've faced childhood wounds I didn't even know I was carrying and I'm learning to sit with my emotions and pain instead of shrinking myself to survive it.

I was angry at my family for a long time. I blamed them for the stress I carried while pregnant. I blamed myself for tolerating it for too long. Did the stress cause Caden's heart to stop? Maybe. I will never know for sure and that is something I have to live with for the rest of my life.

What I do know is this: Caden's life has purpose. I spent my life prioritizing everyone else—absorbing pain, minimizing my needs, staying quiet to keep the peace. Caden changed all of that. His life forced me to face everything I had been avoiding and finally say, *enough*. I stopped abandoning myself and began living in alignment with my truth. He gave me the courage to finally find my voice.

Caden gave me my life, in exchange for his.

While I was pregnant, Chris and I purchased matching t-shirts for the three of us from a company I followed on Instagram. Their designs featured inspiring words woven into beautiful graphic illustrations of animals. Chris and I were drawn to the lion—the one that carried the word, courage.

After giving birth to Caden, the hospital offered us something priceless: a professional photographer who volunteered her time to capture our first—and our last—family photos. We draped Caden's toddler courage shirt across his body and placed a lion stuffed animal beside him. That was the moment the lion became his symbol—and courage became his anthem.

In the months that followed, I grieved with a fierceness that felt too big for words. The grief was consuming, so I returned to the one place where I had always known how to express myself: creating. I'm a potter, and putting my hands back into clay became a lifeline. As I shaped each piece, the tears came freely. I let myself feel everything—grieving the son I longed for and the future I had imagined. And as all of that love and longing for my son poured out of me, it naturally found its way into what I created. I began making hearts—heart bowls in all seven colors of the rainbow, and rainbow heart worry stones etched with words I needed to hold onto, including… *Courage.*

We live in a society that teaches us to run from pain—to suppress it and "move on." But pain doesn't disappear just because we refuse to face it. It lives in the body. It waits. And when it finally demands to be felt, it often shows up in destructive and unhealthy ways.

But the truth I have learned is this: some of the most beautiful, transformative things in life are found on the other side of pain—when we *choose* to sit with it instead of running. When we stop resisting our grief and start listening to it.

Healing requires taking action, and that calls for courage. Courage is turning toward the pain you've been carrying, letting it break you open, and allowing it to lead as you grow and transform. The courage Caden awakened in me continues to guide every step of my journey.

My heart will always ache for my son. I will proudly carry this grief, this *love*, with me for the rest of my life. His life continues through me—in every brave choice I make, in every moment I choose my truth over silence, and in every way I choose to live fiercely because of him.

This is Caden's Courage—and it lives on in every heart brave enough to choose healing.

KRISTINA DEFAZIO-MAMONE

Kristina is an artist who transforms love and loss into handmade creations. After the loss of her son, she turned to creating as a way to process grief—to sit with pain and give it shape. Her work is rooted in the belief that grief is part of being human, and that healing begins when we are brave enough to face what hurts. By turning her grief into something tangible, Kristina hopes to show others that meeting pain with courage can transform how we love, connect, and contribute to our relationships and the world.

CONNECT WITH KRISTINA HERE

www.cadenscourage.com
www.empoweredgriefjourney.com/kristina

Scan to learn more about Kristina

3

WHERE IS THE HOW-TO GUIDE FOR TRAGEDY?

Anne Marie Wells

My father was diagnosed with stage 4 lung cancer in September 2019 after a month-long hospital stay for low blood oxygen levels. That July, I had just landed my dream job working as the executive director for a nature education nonprofit after many years of job-searching and working outside my field to make ends meet in the meantime. I had just been celebrating the greatest win of my professional career, but now I was arranging to work remotely and uprooting my life in Wyoming to move in with my parents on the east coast of Florida to help care for my father and support my mom as she processed her own grief.

Three months after his official diagnosis, my father had undergone one round of chemo and had just started his second, but his body couldn't handle it. The only word I could think of that would have accurately described him in this state was "etiolated," a botany term used to describe a plant that has turned yellow or white, usually due to a lack of sunlight. Since the plant isn't photosynthesizing, it doesn't produce chlorophyll, the component that creates a plant's green color. Because they are forced to search unnaturally for sunlight, the plants become unusually thin as if they have been stretched out. Without any support, the elongated stems eventually collapse on themselves.

So, as tourists and retirees enjoyed cocktails on lanais and watched in awe at the dancing pinks and golds of the sunset, my mother called 9-1-1, and I sped behind my parents in the ambulance to the emergency room. When a nurse brought me to see my father, he lay on a gurney, too weak to even hold an ice chip in his mouth. The assigned nurse couldn't draw blood from his dehydrated veins, and after four failed attempts, called another nurse to try. She then succeeded with smaller needles.

When the doctor finally came hours later to his bedside, my father, whose vocal chords were paralyzed, managed to whisper, "I need a diagnosis. If I'm here only under observation, Medicare won't cover the cost."

"We have a diagnosis, Mr. Wells," the doctor said. "You have pneumonia and sepsis on top of your cancer."

My father was transferred to the hospital's cancer ward. The nurses gave him IV fluids and antibiotics and prepped him for a blood transfusion. Throughout his life, my father was an avid blood and platelet donor, and drove forty-five minutes every six weeks to a Red Cross chapter where he would watch an action film while a tube in each arm extracted the platelets from his blood. When I donated blood for the first time in high school twenty years earlier, I wore his 50-Gallon-Donor pin on my shirt.

"After giving all my blood away, I'm finally going to get some of it back," my father joked.

At 10 p.m., my mother went back to her house to feed the dogs and let them outside. I stayed with my dad on the vinyl loveseat next to his hospital bed. As he slept with the machines humming and whirring around him, a ghost whispered a question in my ear. It asked, "How do you want to remember your father?"

Years earlier, while visiting my parents in Florida, my dad and I were walking a nearby beach as we often did, and we noticed a baby turtle flopping in the sand toward the tide. We stopped to watch it, and then another came, and another, and another. We found the nest and stayed watching the miracle of these reptiles emerging from their sandy wombs until the sun went down. We needed to use my flip phone (no smartphones back then) as a flashlight to make our way back to the parking lot.

I don't have an explanation, but as I lay on the vinyl loveseat next to my unconscious father, the memory of those turtles swirled into my consciousness. Still buzzing with adrenaline and cortisol from that evening, I was compelled to write a poem about my dad and those turtles. The urge felt as strong and as desperate as a hungry person needing to find food, as a freezing person needing to find warmth. I had to write it down. Despite never having written poetry before, I found an old receipt in my bag and walked to the nurse's station to borrow a pen to write the first iteration of my poem, "I Will Remember You This Way, I Promise."

Holding the shell of the man he used to be to my ear,
his tidal voice crashed ashore, calling me
to watch a nest of turtles

break free from their sandy womb, frantic to find
their ocean mother; a race from first breath
to moonlit waves.

I didn't know it at the time, but this was the beginning of an entirely new life. Because I knew a bit about the literary world, I decided to send my poem to some literary journals. To my astonishment, I received my first acceptance email three weeks later. Before my father passed away in February 2020, I was able to tell him about five different poems that were accepted for publication. The day he died, as I silently gave him a sponge bath in his hospice bed, he broke the silence and whispered, "If you want to tell stories about all this, you can."

I resigned from what I thought was my dream job, and after my father passed away, I worked an entry-level position as a caregiver while I went back to school for English, earning an associate's degree in less than a year. I signed up for every free writing class or workshop I could find. Because the Covid-19 pandemic surged shortly after my father passed away, courses that would normally be in person now became available to me virtually in rural Wyoming.

When I'd left Wyoming to care for my father, even though I knew it was impossible, I hoped that somehow I could keep him alive. If I made sure he did his physical therapy, if I made sure he took his medicines, if I made sure he ate well, I could help him stay healthy, and stay with us for longer than his prognoses hinted at. After he passed away, however, I had a new mission: to keep him alive through my writing.

I began work on a memoir-in-verse, *Survived By*, chronicling everything from finding out *the news* to witnessing the many indignities of cancer treatment to watching my hero succumb to the villainous cancer to barely staying afloat through the typhoon of grief to figuring out what healing could look like.

My book *Survived By* begins with these words:

Where is the How-To Guide for tragedy? The textbook for Grief 101? *What to Expect When You're Expecting Someone You Love to Die?*

At the time I was writing it, I really was looking for a how-to guide. I was genuinely asking, "How do I do this?!" How do I watch in anguish as my father loses 100 pounds, loses the ability to walk, and loses the feeling in his hands? How do I bathe and diaper him without him losing his dignity? How do I hold his hand in a room with five nurses bound by my father's Do Not Resuscitate order as he loses his life? I felt like I was steering a plane with no training or air traffic controllers. I needed a guide but didn't know where to turn; The Five Stages of Grief weren't cutting it. No one had any answers, so I had to come up with my own, and I hoped they would someday help others who were trying to fly the airplane of grief, too.

The first step I came up with was to tell everyone to fuck off. And I meant it. I had to fill my circle with only people who made my circle feel full. I gave myself permission to Marie Kondo anyone who wasn't sparking joy in my life.

The second step I came up with was to accept help. Help came from friends, strangers, or anyone. Even if someone I had just cut out of my life reached out to say, "I want to help," I would have pulled out the needle and thread, the super glue, the tape, and found a way to mend the pieces so I could accept that help.

Step three was to cling, and I mean *cling*, to gratitude. I repeated what I was grateful for over and over until the words blurred together and no longer made sense. Even when it felt impossible to imagine having anything to be grateful for, I crawled to gratitude, clung to it like a child would cling to their tattered and milk-stained blanky. It wasn't until I started writing *Survived By* that I understood how much of a gift my grief was. Or rather, not the grief itself, but what the grief symbolized. One of my "glimmers of gratitude" was that I loved my dad. I know so many people who have horrid parents, who are estranged from their abusive caregivers, or for whom their parent's death would be a relief. Having grief means that I loved someone so much that their illness, their death, and their unending absence hollowed me. That love is the gift. I'm grateful for it. I clung and still cling to that glimmer of gratitude.

The fourth step was to find control. My father dying was completely out of my control, so I had to find control somewhere else. I controlled my breath. I controlled saying "hi" with a smile to anyone I passed by. I controlled telling my dad I loved him every day. I controlled how I treated myself. I controlled brushing my teeth, showering, and putting on clean clothes. Though she didn't realize she was doing it, my mother found control via the bathroom counter. She wanted it to be completely free from any sign that someone may have used it. No toothbrush on the sink, no hair ties, no face creams. Nothing. It made no sense to me, but you know what? Having just a little bit to feel in control of can be the difference between treading water and drowning.

Step five was to remember. The ancient Greek poet Sappho once said that whatever could not be spoken would be wept. I knew numbing, ostriching, and disassociating would only make grieving that much harder. The only way forward would be through. I remembered car rides to and from my university. I remembered the way my dad unapologetically wept at the airport when I left on a summer-long trip when I was fifteen. I remembered how he would always give me a little shake at the end of a hug. And I wept and I wept as I remembered and remembered. And eventually as I remembered and wept, I started remembering, weeping, and smiling.

Step six was just chaotically repeating all of the previous steps. One moment I would be telling people to fuck off and the next I'd be accepting help from those same people. I would cling to gratitude, remember something funny he said or did, then grasp to maintain control over something inane before telling someone to fuck off again. I was chaotic, but that's how grief so often is.

Then, after spending a couple years navigating the emotional mess of loss, I realized that I had begun healing. I had reached the seventh and final step that I never thought I would reach. It felt so impossible, and when I was deep in the trenches of bereavement, I had wondered if healing meant that I stopped caring, that I stopped hurting, that healing meant that my dad's death no longer meant anything to me. Now I know that, of course, that's not true. It's been five years since my dad passed away, and there are still days when I cry. I'm crying right now as I write these words. Usually I cry because of something that reminds me of him: his birthday, the anniversary of his death, a photo, a song. But other times, there's no reason. Only a few weeks ago, I was walking home after dropping my car off at the mechanic, and out of nowhere I missed my dad. I cried the rest of the way home. When I walked into my house, my husband asked me, "Oh my God, what happened? Are you okay?" And I just said, "I miss my dad."

If I could re-write my book (and maybe someday I will), I would add a step in between chaotically repeating and healing: finding a purpose. Purpose, in my opinion, was the greatest conduit to my healing. In fact, there is even scientific research that suggests finding a purpose can help mend a broken heart. In her book *Heartbreak: A Personal and Scientific Journey*, nonfiction writer and journalist Florence Williams goes on a quest to heal her broken heart after her husband of twenty-five years asks for a divorce. While reading, I learned that I had unknowingly fulfilled some of the findings: that throwing yourself into a project, a mission, and/or a new identity does wonders for heartbreak. After my father died, I threw myself into writing poetry. I had a new identity: poet. It was the only thing that brought me any kind of solace. Not therapy. Not bereavement group. Not my relationship. Not binge-watching *Schitt's Creek*. Not rice pudding with chocolate chips in it. That's not to say that those other things didn't contribute at all, but writing my story felt like a way for me to keep my father alive, for me to honor our love for one another. You're witnessing this phenomenon right now with this anthology; Chris's way of honoring his son Caden. A friend of mine who discovered her father's bucket list after he passed away went on a quest to complete it for him. I met a man who decided to visit every town in the country called Nelson after his husband named Nelson died from a sudden heart attack. Other people take up knitting or motorcycling. Some people go on a trip they were supposed to take with their loved one. Some people change careers, change cities. Some become sober. Some become religious. And others like me become poets.

If you are drowning in grief, I want to remind you that it's a reflection of your capacity to love, and that is a remarkable strength. I used to think making meaning out of my father's death would mean I was grateful that he died, that I was actually happy about it. And if you're feeling that way, too, I want to discourage you from that line of negative thinking. If you're able to find a purpose as a result of your loss, it only means that you had the courage to face your pain, to sit with it, and to use it to make something beautiful that honors your loved one and makes others who are facing the same kind of pain feel less alone. In the words of the late Carrie Fisher, "Take your broken heart, make it into art." Doing so can only add to the beauty and empathy and light that this world so often lacks, while keeping the memory of your loved one alive and helping you survive the wreckage.

ANNE MARIE WELLS

Anne Marie Wells is an award-winning poet, playwright, memoirist, and oral storyteller. She is the author of two collections of poetry: *Survived By: A Memoir in Verse + Other Poems* published by Curious Corvid Publishing and *Mother Comma Verb*, which won the 2023 Cinnamon Press Chapbook Contest. Her children's book *Mommy, Why Am I a Bird?* was published by University of Coimbra Press and was featured on Wyoming PBS's series called *Story Time With Wyoming Authors.*

CONNECT WITH ANNE MARIE HERE

www.AnneMarieWellsWriter.com

www.empoweredgriefjourney.com/annemariewells

Scan to learn more about Anne Marie

4

HEARTBREAK
THE GRIEF YOU DON'T SEE COMING
Becky Dotson

T here I was, sitting on the couch—the same spot I had been in for days. I hadn't slept. I hadn't showered. I rotated between eating my feelings and starving myself. I tried to numb my emotional pain with alcohol, but that only made things worse. I knew I wasn't dead, but I didn't feel quite alive. Every time I tried to take a deep breath, I felt a pain in my chest so profound that it felt like my heart had actually broken, that it was shattered into a million pieces and there was no way to repair it. I just wanted to cry but there were no tears left, so there I sat just staring at my dog Ollie sound asleep on the end of the couch.… I was a complete wreck.

If it weren't for my dog, I don't know if I would have left the house at all. Ollie needed me, and in that moment, feeling needed was the only thing keeping me breathing.

My thoughts were all over the place.

What did I do wrong? He was supposed to be The One.
Why am I this upset? We were only dating for three months.

And then the real monster crept in with more brutal thoughts.

You're so pathetic.
Seriously?
You thought he was The One?
You're so stupid.

I had never felt this way after a breakup—especially for a relationship that only lasted a few months. Sure, I'd been sad before, maybe cried for a day, drank too much, hooked up with someone else to distract myself. But I would bounce back quickly and usually meet someone new without much effort.

But this… this was different. Every time I attempted to leave my house, I felt sick to my stomach. Everything reminded me of him. The restaurant across the street where we had our first date, the same truck he drove that seemed to be parked around every corner, and walking past families that reminded me of the future we'd talked about but would never have. Seeing these things would instantly make my eyes well up with tears, and I would be forced to retreat to the safety of my couch, which didn't make me forget him but at least I could lose it in private.

And even though I couldn't name it back then, I can now.

It was grief.

I'd started dating this guy—let's call him Mark—three months earlier. We met online and hit it off right away. Our first date turned into an all-night conversation, the kind you see in movies. For the first month, we were inseparable.

He'd show up to my job with sugar-free Red Bulls (my version of flowers); he introduced me to his friends and family; he took care of my dog like Ollie was his own; he planned the cutest dates. He took me to all my favorite restaurants, would drive an hour to see me even if it were only for five minutes, and he would always rearrange his plans to prioritize seeing me. I felt like a princess. He would pay for everything, even taking me to Sephora and let me buy anything I needed to have at his house. Curling irons, hair straightener, make up—you name it, I could have it. He made me feel taken care of, secure, safe, protected—like I was the only girl in the world. For the first time in my life, I felt chosen. It was a fairytale.

We never even had a fight. Things were perfect…

Until they weren't.

About two weeks into our third month, he started pulling away. Slowly at first, but noticeably. He withdrew his attention, affection, and love—and I couldn't understand why. While there wasn't anything overtly wrong, my gut told me something was off. So I decided to bring it up.

"It seems like something's changed," I said. "You've been pulling away. What's going on?"

"This is all in your head," Mark replied. "Nothing has changed. We're fine."

So for the next two weeks, I tried to believe him. I tried to convince myself I was overthinking. I even started questioning my own sanity:

Am I crazy? Do I need to see a therapist?
What did I do to make him act this way?

But deep down, I knew. Something had changed. Eventually, I couldn't take the confusion anymore. So I ended it—and I was devastated. I kept asking myself:

What did I do wrong?
Was he going to come back?
Why did this happen?

I couldn't understand how something so seemingly perfect had completely unraveled.

And so, there I was—again—on the couch, staring at an empty pint of Ben & Jerry's, wondering if I would ever feel normal again. Excited to wake up in the morning to go to the gym and workout with my friends. Happy to take my dog to the park for a walk and soak up some sun. To be able to laugh at a funny movie or to cry tears of joy during the happy ending of a movie. To belt out my favorite country song at the top of my lungs in my crappy beat-up car. To be able to take a deep breath again without it feeling like it could be my last one. I wanted to feel alive.

I tried everything to "feel better," or at least what I thought might help. I jumped back into dating, called up old friends with benefits, went out drinking and partying, hung out with friends, even started therapy. But nothing worked.

Until one day, my roommate made a suggestion. "You should go see my psychic medium life coach."

At the time, I didn't really know what a life coach was, but I did know I liked psychics—and honestly, I was willing to try anything that might bring me some relief from the lackluster, zombie-like existence I felt like I had been living . So I booked an appointment for an hour-long phone call session that would later change the entire trajectory of my life.

For the first time in weeks, I felt a spark of excitement. *Maybe she'll give me hope. Maybe she'll say he misses me and he's coming back.*

After all, I was used to psychics telling me what I wanted to hear about my past heartbreaks. Why would this time be any different?

But this psychic was different. She didn't give me many answers about him at all. Instead, she said something I'll never forget. "You're a gifted psychic. You'll use your gifts one day."

I brushed it off. "Yeah, maybe I'm a little intuitive," I said, "but what about *him*? Is he going to come back? Is he as heartbroken as I am? What should I do?"

She responded gently, "I see that he does this to everyone. It's best to let him go and focus on healing yourself. If he's meant for you, he'll come back."

I won't lie—I was really disappointed in that answer. And to top it off, she gave me... homework. Here's what she assigned:

- Ask your spirit guides to show you who he really is. (Spoiler alert: they did... but that's a story for another time.)
- No dating or hooking up for ninety days. (Hello, Celibate Sally!)
- Journal daily. (The last time I owned a journal it was from Limited Too—kudos if you get the reference.)
- Do one thing every day that brings you joy—she even gave me a list of ideas.
- Go on a solo trip.

We ended the call, and even though it wasn't what I wanted to hear, for the first time since the breakup, I felt something I hadn't in weeks: Hope.

I realized I couldn't force him to come back—no matter how hard I tried. But at least now I had a new kind of challenge, something to focus on other than heartbreak. And so I did it—I completed every single homework assignment for the next ninety days. And here's what happened…

- I learned more about myself than I ever had before— especially about the abandonment wound I'd been carrying since childhood, the one that kept drawing me to men who would ultimately leave me.
- I started putting myself first for the very first time in my life.
- I reconnected with the things I used to love—fitness, friends, and work—and I discovered new passions that truly filled me up: traveling, reading, and writing.
- I began to enjoy being single. (Okay… that one took a few more years to really stick, but the shift had started.)
- I became more grateful, hopeful, and genuinely joyful.
- I started opening up to my psychic gifts—and eventually turned them into a psychic medium business.
- I began to heal—from the inside out. That healing continued over the next few years and still evolves today.
- And, yes… Mark came back. But this time, I saw the truth. This wasn't someone who truly loved me. This was a love-bombing narcissist. And the best part? I didn't want him anymore.

While I wasn't magically healed in just 90 days, that season marked the beginning of an epic healing journey—one I'm still on today.

And what that chapter of my life taught me most is this: Grief comes in many forms. And the only way out of grief…is through it. You have to feel it all.

Sit with it.
Let it wash over you.
Let it teach you.
Let yourself cry.
Let yourself laugh.
Let yourself feel angry, disappointed, hurt, and sad.
Let it be messy.

But the one thing you should never do is judge your grief. Whether you're grieving a breakup after three months or thirty years—it doesn't matter. Your grief is valid, and it's yours. The loss of a relationship can be just as profound as a physical loss.

Take it from me… I'm a psychic medium.

If you had told me back then—curled up on the couch, heartbroken and lost—that this experience would be the doorway to my healing, my purpose, and a completely new version of myself, I never would've believed you. But that's the thing about life: sometimes what feels like the end is actually a beginning in disguise.

Breakups can feel like they're shattering us, but sometimes they're breaking us open—to truth, to growth, to self-love, to our gifts, and to the version of ourselves we were always meant to become. That relationship wasn't a mistake. It was a mirror. A wake-up call. A sacred invitation back to myself.

If you're walking through heartbreak right now, I want you to know this: you're not broken. You're breaking open. You don't need to rush to "get over it." You don't need to shame yourself for how long it's taking. What you need is grace. Gentleness. Space to feel and space to rise.

Let your grief lead you back home to you. Because one day, you'll look back at this moment—not with pain, but with power—and realize that it was the beginning of everything you were always meant for. And you'll finally understand…

You were never losing love.
You were learning to become it.

BECKY DOTSON

With over five years of experience as a psychic medium, Becky helps people heal through deep spiritual connection and intuitive insight. Delivering clear, compassionate messages from loved ones who have passed, she offers comfort, clarity, and guidance to those navigating grief, life transitions, or spiritual awakening. Her gift serves as a bridge between worlds—bringing peace, validation, and a reminder that love never dies.

CONNECT WITH BECKY HERE

www.dogmommedium.com
www.empoweredgriefjourney.com/beckydotson

Scan to learn more about Becky

5

LOVE BEYOND THE VEIL
THE BEGINNING OF OUR ETERNAL BOND

Terri-Ann Russell

One single knock at the front door changed our lives forever. That's all it took to dismantle the world I knew. My adult son Anthony was gone. The police officer's voice still echoes in my mind today. I remember the pain in my heart that followed, so loud it pressed against my ears. My knees buckled. My breath stopped. I fell to the floor screaming so loud, but I couldn't even hear it. It felt like the earth opened beneath me and swallowed everything that I thought was real. Time broke open, and I fell through it. It was like I left my body and was not even in the room. This feeling was quite familiar to me; I've felt it before when trauma had entrenched my life. This time was the worst—I remember being numb, zoned out. There, but not really there.

Three days before he died, I felt guided to visit Anthony. Our entire family—my husband, daughters, and parents—piled into the car to make the trip three hours away. We surprised him with a visit and spent the day with him. I am so grateful we got to spend that time with him. There were no warning signs, no indication he was sick. The only thing that he said to us was that he was a little tired, since he had been working a lot. Later, we found out from the coroner that he died of a medical complication: his pancreas became necrotic and wrapped around his spleen, causing it to burst and bleed internally. He had gone to the hospital earlier that day and had been misdiagnosed with a stomach bug. Within hours, he was gone.

I didn't just lose my son, I also lost myself, "who I was, who I thought I would always be." But what I didn't know then, and what I've come to understand now, is that this loss wasn't an ending. It was the beginning of a different kind of relationship, and the start of a sacred path I never asked to walk but one that would lead me to discover who I truly am.

There are no maps to navigate the season of grief. No road signs. No compass to follow. Just a shattered heart and a mental fog so thick I could barely see my own hands in front of me. In the midst of this fog, I was dazed, confused, and broken. After Anthony died, I entered a realm I had only ever glimpsed in other people's pain. Now, it was my turn to navigate this path for myself; after all this was my child, my boy. He was gone, gone from the physical world, and every cell in my body screamed against it. In the days after his transition, I felt like I was moving through molasses. Heavy. Slow. Dying inside myself. Everything around me looked the same, but I wasn't the same. I was cracked wide open, and the pieces of me that once made sense no longer fit together. I cried so hard some nights that I didn't think I'd survive. My throat would burn. My chest would tighten; it felt as if someone had been sitting on my chest. Grief had moved in—a new, permanent resident in my soul.

People say grief comes in stages. That sounds so tidy. So manageable, like you package it up and feel one way one day and something else the next, but real grief is messy. It's not linear. It doesn't follow logic. It crashes into you like a tidal wave when you're least expecting it—browsing at the grocery store, driving in the car, smelling his favorite cereal—a memory flashes in. *He should be here!* Seeing mothers with their sons and wondering why mine had to go. Heartbroken, I retreated.

Emotionally, I felt everything and I felt nothing, sometimes at the same time. I was numb to everything and anything that required my attention, but I could barely function. There were moments I raged at God. Only another person who has experienced this pain could recognize the wails that came from me. I questioned everything I believed.

I begged God to take me instead. *Let him live and take me.* Why him? Why my child? I was angry, gutted, and inconsolable. But beneath the rage was a sorrow so deep that it carved caverns in my heart. I missed Anthony's voice. His hugs. The way he said "I love you" without needing a reason. The silence where he used to be was unbearable, and the constant ache in my heart persisted. When I say you can truly die of a broken heart, I now understand why.

Physically, my body carried the weight of my sorrow. My bones ached. My head pounded. My appetite disappeared, and sleep became something unreachable. When I did sleep, I'd wake in a panic, gasping for breath, forgetting for a split second, then remembering with a crushing thud. He was gone. Again. Over and over, each morning felt like losing him all over again. I worried that my other grown children, Erich, Tyler, and Sophia would meet the same demise. If this man, my child, a happy, healthy twenty-seven-year-old could suddenly die, then what was to stop another one of my children dying? I became entrenched in fear.

Spiritually, I was both broken and strangely awake. In the beginning, I felt abandoned by God, by the universe, even by Anthony. I begged him to come back to me. I would sit in the dark and whisper, *Where are you? I can't believe you're dead!* Suddenly, without hesitation, I would hear a whisper, *I am not dead. I have gone ahead, but we are still connected.* I needed signs. These signs and messages would be my saving grace. And slowly, as he began to answer, I found the proof that I was looking for and needed so desperately.

At first, it was small bits and pieces, like hearing his voice inside my head, finding random dimes, and having monthly dream visits. Dreams so vivid that I'd wake up still feeling his presence with me. This continued for fifty-two dream visits, all fully documented in my notes. (I still have yet to write a book about that, but I do hope it's coming!) There was one night I felt someone bang the bed and wake me up. I heard him laugh, and I knew it wasn't my imagination. It was him. He was reaching out. It was reassuring to me to know we have this connection, and it gave me faith that one day we would be together again. And I started to understand Anthony hadn't left me. He had simply shifted forms. There was so much to learn; I dove in and found that the more I relaxed my mind with meditation and my body with Reiki, the better I began to feel. It wasn't meant to relieve my pain but rather to help me understand my journey of grief. This journey would unravel over time and expand me in ways I never thought imaginable. This journey is still unraveling today.

I began writing, which I found cathartic. It helped me ease some of the heavy pain that I kept inside of me. Before long, he guided me to write a book, and before I knew it, I had a whole book written. Anthony was amazing; he directed me to my publisher, and she published my first book, *From Death to Life: The Incredible True Story of Anthony Joseph.*

While all of this was reassuring and comforting, it didn't make the pain disappear, but it gave me something to hold onto. A thread of light in the darkness. I began to write down the messages I received. As I'd sit quietly, breathing deeply, and ask, "What do you want me to know, Anthony?" the words would come, not from my mind, but from a deeper place. A place of pure love. The season of grief taught me that healing doesn't mean forgetting. It doesn't mean "getting over it." It doesn't mean moving on—after all, how could I move on from my child? This was not possible. I had to learn a new way to exist with this new relationship we were having. Healing means learning to live with the loss, not in spite of it. It means letting love reshape you in the fire of what has been taken. And I was being reshaped every single day.

Grief became a doorway. A doorway to the unknown, and this sacred initiation would call me deeply into a new phase of my life. It called me into a higher awareness of what It means to love, to lose, and to live again. I could no longer be who I thought I was, but I needed to let go and become who I was always destined to be.

Some days, grief meant that I would stay in bed, wrapped in his purple plaid shirt with the cutoff sleeves, surrounded by his pictures. Other days, grief meant that I forced myself into the world, even if I still felt hollow inside. People didn't always know what to say, and often they said the wrong things. "He's in a better place." "At least you had him for as long as you did." Quite honestly, these words stabbed more than they soothed. What I really needed was someone to just sit with me in my pain. To say, "I see you. I'm here and I hold you within my heart."

I began to understand that Anthony's death had a purpose, not in a way that justified the pain, but in a way that gave it meaning. His soul had chosen this exit point. And my soul had chosen to mother him, even through death. We had switched places, as he told me. He would now be the teacher. I saw him in full apparition one day in my bedroom, sitting in the lotus position, and he would continue to say that now he was the teacher. I taught him, and now it was his turn to teach me.

Healing is not a one and done thing you do. I didn't wake up one day and suddenly say I am "healed." The truth is that there were no lightning bolts of clarity or instant awakenings. It was quieter than those—more like subtle shifts, one after the other, that slowly began to change the landscape of my grief. Looking back now, I can see how each moment, each turning point, was part of a divine orchestration. I didn't know it then, but my healing had already begun, even as I was still buried in pain. One of the first turning points came the day I felt Anthony's energy in the room, which for me was the night he died. I was sobbing, completely undone, whispering, "I can't do this. I don't know how to live without you." And then, the air around me shifted. It felt lighter. Warmer. And in the stillness, I felt him not in body, but in presence. It was unmistakable.

A wave of peace settled over me, just for a moment. A presence full of love. I knew it was him. I didn't hear any words except, "I'm okay, Ma. I'm okay." Years later, as I write, I still cry the pain in my heart that I will hold until I leave the Earth. I had to learn to stop begging for him to return and start learning how to meet him where he was. I surrendered to what this new relationship would be. Spiritual practices also became lifelines—this was what I needed, these daily anchors that pulled me back to center when the waves of despair threatened to drown me. Reiki, which I had already studied before Anthony's death, took on a whole new meaning. It became a pathway to connect with him. Every time I placed my hands over my heart and invited in healing energy, I could feel his soul drawing near.

Reiki wasn't just a healing modality anymore—it was a bridge between worlds. Another profound shift came through my writing. At first, I wrote just to survive. Pages filled with raw emotion, rage, love, questions. I didn't care how it sounded; I just needed to get the pain out of my body and onto the page. But over time, the writing began to change. It became cathartic. It began to heal me. I wasn't just pouring out my grief; I was beginning to listen. Insights began to arrive. Messages. Whispers from Anthony. My writing transformed into a conversation between our souls. He was guiding me and directing the way.

And while these shifts didn't remove the pain, they began to transform it. Pain led to purpose. Sorrow gave way to sacredness. I stopped asking "Why did this happen to me?" and began to ask, "How can this be used through me?" That's when the real healing began.

Today, I am not the woman I was before Anthony transitioned. I am softer. Stronger. Wiser. I carry both the wound and the wisdom. My son's death was not the end of our story—it was the beginning of a new relationship, one that transcends space and time.

The version of me that writes these words today is not the same woman who wept on the bathroom floor begging the Universe to take the pain away, to give me my child back in exchange for my life instead. I am not that same mother, not that same soul. Something in me died when Anthony left his body, but something else was born. Grief was the great destroyer, but also the great awakener. In time, I came to understand that Anthony's passing wasn't the end of our connection. It was a doorway. One that cracked me open to a new world, a world that was filled with spirit, energy, and eternal love. This doorway required everything I thought I was to be burned away. The person I used to be before grief couldn't walk through it. She had to be transformed.

Through the sacred work of unlearning, my healing would begin. It didn't just come from feeling the pain, it came from unlearning everything I'd ever been taught about death, loss, worthiness, and God. Our society doesn't teach us how to grieve. It teaches us to hide, to suppress, to perform. I realized I had inherited beliefs that kept me stuck in shame and suffering. The same shame and suffering that had kept me where I was before. The beliefs included, *be strong, show no emotion, time heals all wounds, grief is something that you get over, you have to move on.* None of what I was told as a child and none of what I was told now was true. Not one single bit of it.

It would take deconstructing those false stories layer-by-layer, piece-by-piece, and then revisiting them again and again. It wasn't easy. It took radical honesty, deep energetic healing, and a fierce commitment to my soul's liberation. Once I began the process of clearing out the conditioned beliefs, something miraculous happened. I could completely hear the truth underneath the noise.

The truth is that grief is love with nowhere to go, until we learn to channel it. That's when I knew I was being called to help others. My pain became purposeful. I began to hold space for those navigating their own storms—not from a place of having it all figured out, but from the deep, embodied knowing of what it's like to feel shattered and still choose to rise.

Today, I guide others through their own grief journeys—not just the loss of a loved one, but the death of identity, the crumbling of illusions, the unraveling of everything they thought they had to be. I call it sacred alchemy. Through Reiki, spiritual hypnosis, somatic experiencing, and intuitive coaching, I help people release the conditioned beliefs that keep them trapped in suffering. Beliefs that tell them they're not enough. Beliefs that they should be over it by now, that they're broken. That they can't feel joy and grief at the same time. I help them remember their truth. Together, we rewrite the narrative. We return to the body. We connect with their loved ones in spirit. We clear lifetimes of ancestral patterns. We come home, not to who they were, but to who they are becoming. Every session is an invitation back to the heart. And every client I work with reminds me that grief is not a curse—it's a calling.

If you're reading this and wondering how you'll survive what feels unsurvivable, I want you to know something: You already are. You may not feel strong or spiritual. You may be angry at God, numb, exhausted, or questioning everything. That's okay. You don't have to be okay to be healing. You don't have to "move on." You only have to keep breathing. Grief is not a detour on your spiritual path—it is the path. Let it break you open. Let it reveal the depth of your love. Let it burn away what no longer serves you. And when you're ready, let it awaken your power to transform. Your grief has a purpose. So does your healing. And so do you. I am walking proof that something beautiful can be born from ashes. That a broken heart can become an open heart. That love never dies. And that connection, when rooted in the soul, is eternal. Anthony and I are still on this journey together. He teaches me from spirit. I share those teachings with the world. Together, we rise. And now, dear one—so will you.

TERRI-ANN RUSSELL

Terri-Ann Russell is a Reiki master teacher, spiritual activator, and author of three books. She is a transformative healer and author whose works offer profound insights into life, death, and the soul's eternal journey. She examines the connections of past lives to this current life. Her writing career began after the sudden and heartbreaking loss of her beloved son Anthony Joseph. This life-altering event sparked a deeper exploration into spiritual healing and life after death.

CONNECT WITH TERRI-ANN HERE

https://linktr.ee/TerriAnnRussell

www.empoweredgriefjourney.com/terri

Scan to learn more about Terri-Ann

6

THE DAY MY INNOCENCE DIED

RJ Fisher

When I was twenty-seven years old, my ex-boyfriend held me hostage in my apartment for six frozen hours. Not wanting to die alone, he was determined to take me with him. Even as he held the knife blade to my throat, I couldn't believe it was happening. Even as I sat zip-tied on my couch, my face stained with tears and mace, my hands bleeding and my head throbbing, I still couldn't believe it. Even as he explained to me how and when I was going to die, I couldn't believe it. *How could this happen to me? Why?*

There are moments in our lives that define us. Life stops you dead in your tracks, like a sucker punch from behind and you stand there blankly staring at your dreams as they vanish. All the happiness. All your innocence. You. Gone. That moment for me came from behind the face of someone I had loved. I never thought a man I had once thought was my soulmate would deem me too evil to live and try to end my life.

Stuck in a deadly chess game, I came face-to-face with everything I stood for and everything I believed. Realizing I was going to die, the most important things in my life became chiseled in vivid colors. *Who would raise my five-year-old son? How would my friends hold on to hope?* I wasn't ready to die yet. What happened that day turned into an epic battle for my mind.

We spent six grueling hours together, struggling with his love and hate for me. Finally, he became distracted scrolling through my cell phone and I was able to flip the lock and run out the door. He chased after me and then disappeared. I went into hiding as the police searched for him. In the early morning hours of the next day, I was told he had been found an hour away, wandering the streets and mumbling to himself. My ordeal was over.

Even though I ended up escaping, my mind remained restrained by fear and self-doubt. I knew the truth, but I believed the lie. My innocence died that day. My trust died and I lost myself. The old RJ was gone and an empty shell was left.

In the days, weeks, and months after he held me hostage, I felt detached from everything and everyone around me. I remember sitting at a table with my friends and feeling like I was watching from the outside. When your body first experiences heavy grief, the normal everyday things become nothing. All you can think about is life and death and loss. And that doesn't make for good dinner conversation.

I started to isolate myself. No one knew what I was actually going through. I have never felt anything quite like it before or since. I felt empty and sad and scared all at once all the time. I found a blank space in my mind to escape to, where I could watch the world from outside. As soon as I was alone with my thoughts, I fell apart. I drank alcohol trying to find relief. Sometimes that relief never came. As soon as my eyes closed, I had nightmares and would jump awake in a sweat. I would call my brother in the middle of the night, crying and asking the big question: *Why?* This continued for several years.

Fear was as tangible as the grass beneath my feet. I could feel it. Taste it. It was always with me. Looming like an old, unwanted enemy. I was afraid to be happy. I was afraid to relax for even one second. I was afraid of the man sitting on a park bench. I was afraid of people who "cared about me." I was afraid to walk through any city. I was afraid of an unfamiliar grocery store.

I rarely slept. If I did, it was because my body had finally passed out in utter exhaustion. I was always alert. I rested sitting up, listening to every sound. The world was menacing now. Fear called the shots, like a cruel, demanding overlord. Physically, my body was in overdrive. I was constantly busy. Afraid to rest for the thoughts that would come tumbling down on me. I stayed up all night. I exercised hard.

My body reveled in overdrive, bringing an exhausting, sweet release to my mind. On the outside, I looked like I was alright. No one saw me falling apart. No one saw me scared. I was rather legendary—I made sure I excelled at work and at being a mom. No one could see me falter. Inside, I was cracking. Holding on by a thread. Memory loss. Brain fog. Disorientation. Numbness. Shaking. Panicking. I needed help, but I didn't know where to go, and the world wasn't stopping for me to figure it out.

Safety was my number one, primal instinct. My body craved safety like it was the last oxygen on Earth. Nothing else mattered. I didn't care if anyone loved me. I didn't care if anyone wanted me.

I wanted to be safe. I could never be home alone. On nights when my son wasn't there, I would sleep in my car. I bought a guard dog and a gun. I hung out with people who promised to keep me safe, disregarding whether they were good for me or not. I poured everything into building a fortress out of my life.

I did not let anyone get close to me. Sure, I loved others and gave them my all, but I never let anyone know who I really was. I was the perfect friend—I gave everything and asked for nothing. People took advantage of my silence, but I didn't mind. I exchanged my authenticity for safety.

After all, I thought no one wanted the real me anyway. I buried her deep inside and focused on survival. I thought if I was just beautiful enough! If I was just smart enough! Capable enough! I would be worthy of love. I stopped eating to be skinnier. I took risks. If I could just be enough! Time after time, I thought I found people to stand in my corner, only to be left standing alone. And now, here I was, bleeding out because my ex had deemed me "too evil to live." I was done.

Six months after the hostage situation, I sat in my car parked at an old cemetery. The sun was setting. I was listening to "The Wrong Side of Heaven" by Five Finger Death Punch. Tears rolled down my face. I was tired of being afraid. I was tired of being alone. I was tired of being a burden to everyone. I couldn't detach anymore. I didn't want to be afraid. I stuffed a sponge in my tailpipe and closed my eyes to sleep forever. I was completely broken.

Thankfully, I awoke later to a clear tailpipe and a cool breeze. It wasn't my time to go. I had been given yet another chance. I knew I couldn't live this way anymore. I needed answers. I needed to climb out. I wanted to live. And so, began my search for healing.

My journey to find myself again.

I didn't realize it at the time, but I was grieving the loss of the innocence I had before that day. I had been vibrant and friendly, dubbed a "social butterfly" by all who knew me. I was bold and never afraid of my surroundings. If there was one girl in the group who would take the risk and blaze the trail, that was me. I was fearless. The girl who looked back at me in the mirror now was buried in the grief of lost love and security. My heart was purely broken.

I'd like to say that after my breakdown I reached out for help, but the cruel irony of being hurt by someone close to you is that you think no one is safe. However, I knew I needed to pull myself together. I had to gain control of my emotions or they were going to kill me. So, I set out on a journey to control my mind. I wanted to be in control of my monsters and my actions.

Panic attacks came first. How on earth could I gain control of my mind when it was automatically shutting down? I knew there were warning signs before an impending attack. If I could predict when they were going to happen, I could stop them before a complete shutdown. I put safety-inducing options in place. If I was home, I went somewhere I felt safe, which for me, was my car or the nearby cemetery. I would feel the earth with my fingers and concentrate on the tangible sensation.

With a pre-plan in place, I knew what to do when I felt the familiar tightness in my chest and tremor in my hands. Stopping a panic attack before it started was half the battle. I learned to guard my time and space like they were precious treasures. I figured out what recharges my emotional batteries and made sure that was my number one priority.

For me, it's time alone. Time to think, journal, walk, and just sit quietly with my thoughts. If I don't do this regularly, I will be certain to fall apart at some point during the week. What is real? How much of the thing we fear is perception? Draw a monster. Now, look at it and ask, "What makes it a monster?" An encounter with death will bring anyone to their knees. Step back and look at the thing you fear. Ask yourself why. I realized that my real fear is being powerless.

I had to identify what was real. Was there really a monster lurking in the shadows to destroy me or was it a human being with a broken mind? Is it possible that healing could happen on both sides and the fear could be resolved? If redemption could be achieved, my pain would be worth something. This reality became my saving grace.

Life is unknown. Happiness happens. Pain happens. None of us avoid either of them. To give fear control over our decisions is to quit living. The dance is intricate and confusing, but the reality is that everything has its place and time. I accepted life as the reality that it is, but where was my place in it? Who was RJ now? I would find her later, quietly waiting in the shadows.

She was creative. She appreciated the intelligent, purposeful design in everything around her. She was free. And in that freedom, I looked around and saw the scars of generation after generation of pain handed down. I saw how people lash out at others because hurt is all they know. I knew it was my purpose to awaken people to their full potential outside the pain.

I obtained a position working inside the prison system, and I now impact the lives of inmates on a daily basis. They know my story. They know how their actions have broken people. Who better than someone who can walk between the world of the victim and the world of the predator? Evil doesn't stop if we ignore it. My passion for a solution and my pain came together in a powerful drive impossible to ignore. I had to redefine who I had become. I am now a leader in social change.

Once I saw reality for what it is and knew myself as I really am, everything fell into place. Suddenly, all the problems in life became manageable. They were merely steps to a bigger goal. I could see outside the tiny box that was my life to the bigger picture of the universe. Today, I am free. From the person I was before that fateful day to the person I am today, I found my place in this world. I know who I am. I know where I belong. I know the impact I want to make in this world.

Today, I know how to regulate my emotions. I know how to step back from situations and figure out what's going on. I can regulate fear and panic and channel it to an outlet. The fight never goes away, but I get stronger every time. I still have bad days. I have moments when I grieve. Moments when I doubt myself. I let the anguish wash over me, I have a good cry, then I pick myself up, brush the dirt off, and take the next step forward.

Two darkest times stand out: A month after that cataclysmic day, my son went to the hospital for a minor injury. I've never felt so numb, alone, or broken. I was exhausted. At my wits' end. Completely terrified of what the universe would throw at me next. A second bleak time was that day at the cemetery when I gave up. The weight of all the pain won that day. Anything after that has less force than the torrent of emotions on those days. I know that if I could muscle through those awful moments, I am strong enough for anything that might occur afterward.

Grief gave me a door into the souls of others. I know loss. I know pain. I know betrayal. On the deepest level. I understand people who are suffering, and I know they just need someone to sit next to and be okay with. Grief taught me the value of life. Every moment, every second, every opportunity is precious. All the time you get to have is invaluable.

Watching my son graduate from high school was deep and beautiful for me because at one point, that was all I prayed for. Not only was my prayer to see him grow up answered, but I have been given a man to help me learn to trust again and more incredible children. Love does not come easy. I never in a million years would have thought that I would be sitting where I am today, smiling and gazing out on the rolling woods of my backyard.

If you are reading this, you have most likely experienced grief. You are all too familiar with that tearing feeling in your soul. The nights of silent screams and tear-soaked pillows, when all you want is for things to go back to the way they were. All you want is that person back. Your joy, your hope, your future to be returned to you. You want life to make sense again and not be some dark, ominous, confusing void. You feel lost in your pain.

No one can truly understand how precious your loss is. That it was your world. I see you. I feel you. It hurts. It hurts so bad. It's okay. Let your pain out. Cry, yell, punch the sky. Instead of pushing the pain away, push deeper into it until you can't breathe. Scream at it and rage against its cruelty. Then, let it go. Mourn the beauty of what you have lost. Sit there in this moment. Let the tears roll down your cheeks.

Now, wipe your eyes and listen. Your story is not over. You still have many beautiful things to see and beautiful souls to touch. Now, you understand how amazing and wonderful life can be. Now, every moment is going to be touched with meaning and depth. And now, you join the ranks of those who have been forged through fire. We welcome you into the sacred circle of knowing. Come honor what we have lost with us. Their memory is a beacon of hope and light. A reminder of how precious life is. Build a legacy out of the ashes of your heartbreak. Who knows? Perhaps our grief will change the world forever.

RJ FISHER

RJ Fisher works within the prison system as a writer, qualitative researcher, and motivational speaker. Her true crime novel *The Girl That Got Out* explores the six hours her ex-boyfriend held her hostage and her recovery from the emotional trauma that event caused her. RJ holds a degree in Criminal Justice from Penn State, studied Urban Ministry at Moody Bible Institute, and has worked in the fields of urban solutions, archaeology, and mental health. She lives in the woods with her significant other and their six children. Her motto is: Be Better, Do Different.

CONNECT WITH RJ HERE

www.girlthatgotout.com

www.empoweredgriefjourney.com/rjfisher

Scan to learn more about RJ

7

YOUR GRIEF WILL
WAIT FOR YOU

Jillene Fritch-Gallatin

My mom, Mina Jean Fritch, died by suicide when I was fourteen years old. By nature, I am a helper. I've known this since I was very young—before Dad's drinking got out of hand, before Mom and I moved to a one-room apartment at the time of Mom and Dad's separation, before Mom died.

Since Mom died when I was living with her, I told myself her suicide was my fault. I was traumatized by my defect in being able to help others but not my own mother.

It was the middle of March, and spring was taking its time to arrive. The days were damp, and the sun struggled to offer warmth through gray skies. Mom's final week started with a phone call on a Saturday morning.

I can still see her cowered at the kitchen table of the apartment we'd moved into eight months earlier. She was wearing her white-

and-pastel striped bathrobe, her forehead resting in one hand, phone gripped in the other, legs tightly crossed, several Marlboro butts discarded in an overfull ash tray. I heard her boss screaming at her through the receiver, and her body resembled her spirit: small and crushed.

She briefly looked up at me.

Hang up, I mouthed.

She quickly looked away. The voice continued yelling through the phone receiver. I froze with fear. Consumed with desperation, I audibly pleaded, "Hang up!" knowing the caller wouldn't hear me over his excessive reprimand.

I pieced together that the real estate firm Mom helped run was about to get bad press in the city's biggest newspaper—all because she forgot to pay a bill or something. Since she was second-in-charge, it was a serious oversight, and her boss was furious. She had made a big mistake—but people's lives don't need to end because of a mistake.

Logically, I comprehend that Mom had a lot going on: moving forward from a failed marriage, living with chronic headaches, navigating a bout of bronchitis, and trying to recover from a major error at work. She often had a lot going on, but she'd always gotten through tough times before.

The chest virus gripped Mom with a cough that worsened throughout the week. She was a smoker, so she often coughed, but these jags were different.

Her only grandchild was turning a year old, but Mom felt she was too sick to go to the birthday party. We were all shocked when she told us she wasn't going to attend the celebration, but it was Mom—she made things okay, calm, and believable. She explained she wanted to rest and not get anybody else sick. She stayed home;

I went to the party.

The next night's memory is as clear as the palm of my hand. It was Sunday night. I had just turned out the lights to go to sleep when Mom knocked on my bedroom door. I told her she could come in, but she remained in the doorway. The glaring hallway light behind her was an unwelcome intrusion that made it difficult for me to look at the black silhouette of her body.

Continuing the story of her cough, Mom explained that my sister would take me to my scheduled eye doctor appointment the next afternoon. I was fourteen, so I'm sure I made some snarky comments for her to leave, but she lingered in the doorway.

In a calm, matter-of-fact tone she explained that I shouldn't worry if she was gone the next morning. She planned to go into the office before others got there—the same rationale she'd given for skipping the birthday party: she didn't want to expose anyone to what she had. It made sense to me.

She didn't move from the doorway. Why was she just standing there? I said something like, "Okay. Goodnight." After a few more moments, she stepped back into the hallway and closed my door. There is no way I could have ever imagined that would be the last time I'd see my mom alive.

The next morning I woke up. No Mom. I figured she was at work like she said. I went to school.

Later that day, my sister picked me up from school. We didn't go to the doctor; we went to the apartment Mom and I called home. Mom wasn't there. We looked around but didn't see any sign that she'd been there recently. We discovered she never showed up at work.

Trying to make sense of what was happening, my sister and I began going through the apartment. We found car keys. We went to the garage and paused before opening the door.

In those moments, I realized time was moving differently. Fear and hope were meshing together. A gentle fog enveloped my mind, eyes, heart, and limbs. A strange mix of anxious dread shrouded me, like a heavy wet blanket. A part of me wanted to see something—anything—and yet I was afraid of what we might find.

Minutes became weighty, making each breath labored and each blink mechanical. We found no answers but instead were typhooned with horrendous possibilities that started with *Oh, God, no* and *What if?*

Opening the garage door, we found mom's car. Relief. Dread. Fumbling through the keys, we located the one for the trunk. We popped the latch and found the trunk empty. Relief. Dread.

We went back into the apartment. My sister wanted to change out of her work clothes, so we went to my closet. I remember standing in front of tops and pants—whatever fills a fourteen-year-old's closet—and thinking, *Things change from here.* Though physically we were just putting on different clothes, my soul knew this time marked a deep shift.

In that pause, standing beside my sister, helping her find something to wear, I realized a part of me was gone. I couldn't explain it, but I became aware of a chilled emptiness that I had never known before. I tried to ignore it.

My sister left to get her family situated. I was alone in the apartment. I couldn't stay there; I couldn't stay still. I went for a walk. While walking, I noticed the emptiness I first felt standing in front of the closet. It grew and solidified. This feeling was cold and dark. I felt like I was free-falling and I knew I was without a mother. I didn't know how—I didn't know where she was—but the part of me that knew her presence had grown still and quiet. It was like a cocoon was forming around the memories that were my mom and it was now my responsibility to protect it—to keep what was left of her safe. I felt like I had to keep moving for fear the emptiness would consume me.

I returned to the apartment, and my sister arrived shortly afterward. It was the longest night of my life, but finally dawn broke.

The next day dragged on. I stayed with a friend. While I was there, the phone rang. I froze.

My friend's mom answered. She didn't say anything but went to her car. My friend and I followed.

Traffic moved slowly and then halted. Time seemed to stop during that car ride. I wanted to get out of the car and run, but I was paralyzed with fear.

Cars began to crawl forward, including ours. We arrived at the apartment building. A police car was parked outside, and I remained in the car, unable to move. Sitting there, I noticed a woman wearing mom's mint-green jacket sitting in the backseat of the cop car.

For a few brief moments, I thought, *She's okay—Mom's here. Everything will be okay.*

My feeling of hope was completely hijacked and replaced with panic. I was unable to breathe as the police officer opened the back door of the squad car to let Mom out—only it wasn't Mom; it was my sister. She had been placed in the car so the officer could tell her they found Mom and what had happened: our mother had suicided.

No one ever told me my mom died; instead, I overheard the life-altering news when my sister was on the phone telling our extended family.

In those first few moments of hearing that my mom died—by

her own hand, her own choice, her own plan—the fragile hope that I'd desperately nurtured over the years was shattered. Like the fragile layer of newly formed ice on a pond, my world was instantly smashed: Crushed was the hope of Dad sobering up for good. Decimated was the hope that Mom would be happy. Evaporated was the hope that I'd be safe and cared for. Severed was the hope of being a family—all my delicate longing for a better future was obliterated with the news of Mom's decision. Her leaving me severed the tether of my security, and what remained were jagged shards of betrayal, abandonment, and fear.

Feeling like I was looking in on someone else's tragic life, I wanted to escape. The closest thing I could do was go to my room to pack. I didn't know where I would be going, but I knew I wouldn't stay in the little apartment that had become our home.

Within a week, I moved "home," back to the house Mom and I had moved away from eight months earlier when she left her husband. Dad had completed treatment and was intent on maintaining sobriety now that he had a new lease on life. He was moving forward, but my mom was dead. I was filled with rage and fear. I was so alone. I felt like no stable adult was around to help me sort out the hell my life had become.

Looking back on those first few years after Mom died, I believe everyone did the best they could. Dad suddenly had a teenager under his roof and needed to provide for us on one income. My sister was navigating her own young family life, yet still welcomed me in her home. Other people were palpably uncomfortable when I was around. What do you say to a fourteen-year-old whose mom took her own life?! My friends were more consumed with what sweater to wear instead of needing to find dinner for themselves again. To say I felt alone does not even come close to the depth of isolation my heart grappled with. I constantly felt frantic, except when I was at church.

Part of my dad's recovery involved going to church every Sunday. During his drinking days, we made it to the occasional Easter or Christmas services. Now we were regulars, which was good.

Pastor Blair knew I was angry, and he was okay with it. He helped me consider that I might be mad at God. I didn't know that was an option until Blair encouraged me to "tell God how I felt."

I wasn't sure about that, but one afternoon I went into the sanctuary and yelled—and cried—and pounded the floor. Exhausted, I laid beside the altar and wept for a long, long time.

In the twenty-eight years that followed Mom's death, I graduated from high school and college, traveled around the US, Europe, and China, earned a master's degree, got married, had two kids, and became a Lutheran minister.

I made it a part of my life's purpose to figure out why Mom suicided. I thought if I figured that out, then I could help others, even though I had failed my own mother. But I also needed to know why because I was terrified that if I couldn't figure it out, then I could do it, too—I didn't want to cause my family, my friends, or my community the horrendous pain all of us went through years earlier.

The closer I got to Mom's age at her death, the more consumed I became with fear and urgency to find an answer. When I was idle, I felt shrouded with that cold void I first felt at age fourteen when I realized she was gone.

I took up running. My body, my mind, and my soul needed to keep moving. I was afraid to stop—until I had to.

I had a major knee injury three weeks before my first (and only) marathon. Doctors advised me not to run; I did it anyway. In excruciating pain for over half of the event, I got through it.

In the months that followed, my body and mind seemed to unravel. Everything in me pleaded to stop, and I did. I had to. I had a breakdown. I couldn't keep going like I had. I had to pull back, leaving staff and volunteers at Trinity Lutheran Church to pick up the pieces of the mess I made because of my fear, anger, and constant pushing.

My husband and our children took care of everything in our home. People were gracious and kind, helping when and how they could. I felt loved and supported, and I knew I wasn't alone.

It was then that I realized the answer to the question I had been pursuing so long: We are not meant to live in isolation; we are not meant to move through life alone, especially the really hard parts.

With love and support from others, I was able to move through the fear and anger I had suppressed and carried since my childhood. My grief had waited for me.

When I finally stopped running, I heard what my body and mind had been waiting to tell me all along. *Mom's suicide wasn't your fault. You were fourteen. You did the best you could, and it was enough. You are enough.*

I practiced yoga in the years that followed my knee injury. I thought stretching would help my knee recover. But on my yoga mat, I could just "be." I was safe; I could think, feel, cry, and heal. The fear that kept Mom's memories cocooned loosened its grip.

Eight years later, I became a certified yoga teacher. Soon afterward, I discovered Grief Yoga: a practice that uses movement, breath, and sound to release pain and suffering in order to connect with more empowerment and love for ourselves and others. I have been teaching Grief Yoga since 2023.

I became certified as a Grief and Loss Coach in January 2024. As a coach, I recognize that each person is whole, creative, and resourceful. No one is broken, no one needs to be fixed— support is sometimes needed when moving forward.

In July 2024, I founded *Grounded Love for Grief and Loss*, where I offer both Grief Yoga and Grief and Loss Coaching to support people moving forward in their grief.

There is no right or wrong way to move through grief. It's different for everyone. When things come up that you feel like you've already dealt with, it can be frustrating. But being curious as to what you might learn in this time and place can offer another level of healing that you're now ready to embody. Trust yourself. Be gentle with yourself. Though it's your healing journey, you are not alone.

When you connect with people who love you for you, when you have tools and resources to support you, and when you're ready, you will heal. Your grief will wait for you.

JILLENE FRITCH-GALLATIN

Jillene Fritch-Gallatin is the founder of *Grounded Love for Grief and Loss* and an ELCA pastor from Minnesota. Her passion for cultivating compassionate, healing spaces began at age 14, following the suicide of her mother—a loss that shaped her lifelong commitment to fostering connection and support in grief. Through the integration of Grief Yoga and Grief/Loss Coaching, she offers transformative tools to help individuals navigate grief with authenticity, empowerment, and love. Jillene enjoys time outdoors with her spouse Peter, their adult children, and their dog Gus.

CONNECT WITH JILLENE HERE

www.groundedloveforgrief.com

www.empoweredgriefjourney.com/jillene

Scan to learn more about Jillene

8

THE LIFE I NEVER THOUGHT I'D HAVE TO LIVE

JoBeth Polley

I wish I didn't have the experience needed to write this chapter for you. My heart breaks for you, the one who picked it up, hoping to find answers after a loss. I wish we weren't connected in this way. But here we are.

I want to sit with you today as you hurt. I want to show up for you in a way that's helpful. And I want to do that by first letting you know that in the isolating depths of your grief, where you feel so alone, many of us join you. I want to share my story in the hope that it reminds you you're not alone and helps you reconnect with the hope that might feel out of reach right now.

Unlike many girls growing up, I never dreamed of being a mom. I wanted a career—I wanted to be successful. I always desired things as a kid, and even though my family did well financially, I was always looking for more, so I planned to create that for myself in adulthood. I had big plans. But that all changed when I met Travis.

Travis was eight years older than I was. He had an established business. Everyone admired his work ethic. He was generous and focused, and his success as a local contractor was on the rise. I was about to turn eighteen when we met, and we both knew that any plans we had made before were now irrelevant because we would be moving forward together. We had both sworn off marriage. It wasn't appealing to either of us until we met.

Shortly after we met, Travis talked about how he couldn't wait to see me pregnant someday. He longed for family. He wanted to see me as a mother, and for the first time, the idea of being a mom felt so comforting. It felt like a complete life. I could see it. I could see us, and I couldn't wait. I loved him so much, and the thought of having a family with him felt right. Two years later, we got married. Two years after that, his dad's long battle with congestive heart failure was coming to an end. As we cared for him, I watched my husband slowly say goodbye to the man who built him.

During this time, we were also trying to get pregnant. We were close to my sister and her husband and wanted our kids to grow up together, so we tried to get pregnant at the same time. Travis's dad passed away. I felt that a baby would be so healing for Travis, taking on the role of a father as he said goodbye to his own. Months and months went by. Negative pregnancy test after negative test. It didn't make sense. My doctor suggested that we run some diagnostics to determine the cause of the problem. We quickly discovered that having a baby was not going to happen for us. We were devastated.

The next day, my sister stopped by with exciting news. She was pregnant! That was when two strong emotions collided: I was going to be an aunt! And I would never have a baby. Extreme joy for my new role as an aunt and for my sister becoming a mom for the first time mixed with complete devastation, knowing that the closest I would ever get to having a baby was being part of my sister's pregnancy.

In the weeks that followed her announcement, I felt like I was living in two worlds. On the outside, I celebrated with her—sharing in her excitement, I helped pick out things for the baby and dreamed of this new person I would get to love. But privately, I grieved what would never be. Every tiny onesie we folded and every mention of the baby was a beautiful reminder of her joy and my loss. It was a tender, complicated space to stand in, loving her while silently mourning my own dreams.

No doubt, it was hard, but my joy for her remained. Both emotions coexisted, and I'm grateful for that. Still, my emotional pain was real. Her baby shower was the hardest day. Woman after woman placed her hands on my tummy and asked, "You're next, right?" or "When will you have a baby?" I smiled and lied.

On the way home, I broke down crying. My mom didn't know the heartbreaking news, but I finally told her. Only my sister had known until then. I hated seeing Mom hurt. I was already carrying so much distress—I didn't want to hand it to her, either. But she was grieving in her own way, and I was tired of hiding.

My husband and I traveled the country looking for answers. Our last and most heartbreaking attempt was an embryo transfer with three perfect donated embryos. Everything looked ideal. We flew to South Florida, and the night after the transfer, Travis and I walked through downtown Fort Myers. I told him, "It's just the five of us!" It felt certain.

Three days later, I had bloodwork done back home. The next day, while on my break at the school where I worked, I got the call—I wasn't pregnant. I quietly walked across the hall, let another teacher know I was leaving, texted my principal, and went home. I cried myself to sleep. The perfect scenario… ended in failure.

A few months later, we decided to adopt from foster care. It was a noble choice, and we felt confident that God was closing the door on the possibility of pregnancy. We knew we had to accept it and move on. I kept busy. Travis kept busy. I cried a lot. I had been crying for the past three years. I was so tired of feeling sad and disappointed. We understood that pursuing adoption might bring more disappointments, but it was our only option to start a family.

Six months later, we met our kids. They were one and seven at the time. Their life hadn't been going as hoped-for either. We all found each other, four broken hearts that were yearning for family and connection. Travis and I began as babysitters and were later chosen as their adoptive parents. After the court day when we officially became their parents, I finally slept. Our family was complete, and we had two precious kids who would always be ours.

Shortly after adopting the kids, we bought a farm. Travis built our home, including everything we wanted, and left room in the budget for an in-ground pool and a basketball court for the kids. The house was beautiful. We had everything we dreamed of; we had each other, two healthy kids, a small ranch, and new vehicles. I had a promising career in education at the University of Arkansas, and Travis's job was exploding with great opportunities.

We enjoyed our time together. Raising animals on our farm, playing basketball in the front yard, riding the Ranger around the farm, having dinner as a family every night, saying bedtime prayers, and celebrating holidays. Our lives were so rich. There were no gaps. No absences. We went to bed at night with full hearts and a sense of contentment.

I homeschooled our kids so we could spend more time together as a family and so our son could work with Travis. We felt like we had already missed a lot of time with the kids, so we created a life that allowed us to spend as much time with them as possible. Life was good, until it wasn't.

In January 2021, Travis started getting bad headaches to the point that he couldn't get out of bed. I was scared. I thought maybe he had COVID. On my way back from the local pharmacy, I got scared and started to cry. He needed to see a doctor. He hated going to the doctor, so it was a fight to get him there. We stopped by my mom's on the way to the hospital and dropped the kids off. We walked into the urgent care, and they immediately took him back for a CT scan, which revealed a huge mass on the front of his brain. The doctor told us this was serious and we needed to go to the emergency room immediately to get an MRI.

Before we went to the ER, I stepped into the next room and called my dad. I didn't want to be here alone if Travis died, and the doctor gave me reason to think that this was a possibility. Within a couple of hours at the ER, the MRI was finished, and the doctor came to talk to us. The room was dark because the light hurt Travis's eyes. She said the MRI showed he had an aggressive form of brain cancer called glioblastoma and handed us a packet about the deadly disease. At the top, it read, "12–16 month prognosis." My husband only had 12–16 months to live.

We left there with shattered dreams. I didn't even know what life was anymore. Everything that mattered no longer mattered— career, vacations, food—all became insignificant. The only thing that mattered was figuring out how we could save him. I spent the next eight months trying to do just that. I read books and talked to doctors, but hope seemed lost. Still, I kept searching and believing that he would be the one to survive. I clung to hope because it felt so much better than fear. We worked with the best doctors in the United States. Month after month, they told me they couldn't heal him and that they were just giving him more time. But I still believed he would be healed, and saying goodbye was never supposed to be part of our story.

Despite my hope, Travis died a year after his diagnosis. It was strange. For months, I had been grieving the loss of this life we had built. I wanted to stomp my foot like a toddler. I didn't want to do this. I hated my life so much. People came to my house, surrounding me, yet I had never felt so alone. Being out in public broke my heart. Everywhere I looked, I saw families. Mine was broken now. I knew the day he passed that I would spend the rest of my life feeling like something was missing that would never be found. People brought food, donated money, and delivered sympathy cards. But when I walked into my bedroom and shut the door, the cold truth was that I was the only one who could get me through this. At the end of the day, it was just me.

But the story gets better—just kidding, it actually gets worse. After my husband died, I lost most of my other relationships. People started out supportive, but they disappeared quicker than I expected.

I've spent hours wondering why. Some probably thought I was doing fine—because I told them I was. That made it easier for them to walk away. One family friend even said I didn't look like I was grieving. What they didn't know was that I cried on my bathroom floor every night for a year. But perception is reality, and I appeared to be okay.

I also shut people out. I was juggling a farm, a business, a job, two kids, and a shattered heart. I didn't have much energy to give to maintaining previous relationships, even though the relationships were so important to me.

Some people avoided me because they'd made big promises they couldn't keep. Others couldn't handle seeing me without Travis—or with someone new when I remarried a year and a half later.

I think some left because I changed.

I met God in a way I never had before. I left the church I'd been part of for thirty-three years, which strained my relationship with my family. My priorities shifted. I stopped chasing success and started seeing life differently.

I lost my husband and then many of our friends. And things shifted with my family in ways I didn't expect because of choices I had made.

But something beautiful happened along the way.

I discovered who I was and what truly mattered. It came with a lot of loss, and it hurt a lot of people.

I found love again. I was blindsided, but I found someone who is a true partner and the person who will walk with me as we pursue authenticity and embark on a journey to our forever home in heaven.

My faith in Christ was transformed, and I live in His presence, dreaming of the day I will be with Him. I long for the day when I can sit with Him and leave this world behind. I find comfort in the only thing that brings true comfort. Without all this loss in my life, I would not have seen the need for a Savior. And for that, I am thankful.

I made some of the best friends a person could ever ask for. We don't do surface-level talk. We get to be real and honest. Our hearts are connected.

The gifts that come after loss are abundant.

Loss is transformative. And the cool thing is that you get to choose how it transforms you. You can choose to accept it for all the bad that it is and all the pain that it brings. But that doesn't sound like a good option for me. I have hurt enough in this life, and I wonder how much better I can make the rest of it.

Please consider what good can come from your loss. I know "good" may feel out of reach for you right now. And that's okay. Just keep revisiting it, asking—*Can I consider what may be good today?* Do this every day, and then one day, you will see how to support someone else who is suffering from a broken heart.

Or maybe you love more deeply and more authentically—or perhaps you will find your purpose and fulfillment in this next chapter of your life.

My next chapter led me to many things that I love and consider to be most precious in my life. My new friends, my new marriage, my relationship with my kids, my faith, and my new career.

After Travis died, many things felt meaningless. The world didn't look the same anymore. I realized that the pain and suffering I walked through and will continue to walk through is not unique—many people suffer every day from the hurts of this world, whether it be death, divorce, disaster, disease, or something of the like.

I knew as I began the journey that would lead to my husband's death that if I figured out how to survive this, I would help others do the same someday. After his passing, I chose to get certified as a grief recovery specialist, so I could help other people navigate loss. This evidence-based program supports healing in a way that is both effective and emotionally safe. It's been a blessing in my life. I'm not afraid of facing difficult things, which allows me to show up for others when they're going through painful experiences.

I hope you found hope in my story. I'm sorry you're going through something so hard that you might not see a light at the end of the tunnel. Let each day be an opportunity to take a step in the right direction—then eventually you'll start to see glimpses of beauty in a world that has been tarnished by your loss.

JOBETH POLLEY

JoBeth Polley is a certified grief recovery specialist who helps others navigate loss with faith, compassion, and practical tools. After losing her husband to brain cancer, she turned her own pain into purpose by walking with others through grief. JoBeth lives on a farm in Arkansas with her family and believes healing is possible when we make space for both sorrow and hope.

CONNECT WITH JOBETH HERE

www.nwagriefspecialists.com/
www.empoweredgriefjourney.com/jobeth

Scan to learn more about JoBeth

9

RETURN TO THAT HIGH MOUNTAIN

Shaleem Dzon

W hen does grief start? And when does it end? Mine certainly didn't start the day my husband died. It started the day he and I sat side by side in that doctor's office, holding hands and shaking our heads, as the oncologists asked, "Do you have any more questions?" The news was still sinking in. "No treatment options. Three to six months."

The anxiety and stress of watching my best friend and husband die of cancer took its toll, since there is no easy way to navigate a situation like that. It was what the experts call anticipatory grief. But I'll tell you this—there is no way to anticipate how bad it will be when the end comes. All I knew was that I loved him more each day, even as his life was slipping away. Just a year earlier, we were getting married. We were newlyweds, and so in love.

I can still see Brad, the eternal optimist, on his deathbed saying to me, with a far-off smile, "I want my ashes scattered at some beautiful place and high on Mount Hood, like Illumination Rock, along with Marley's ashes. And then, someday," he said calmly looking at me, "you can take Digby's ashes and scatter them there, too."

He died at home in our bed, on a cold January afternoon. And when he took his final breath, my world shattered, and the grief that I faced was traumatic and distressing beyond my wildest dreams—or nightmares. I became a widow when I was forty-five years old in January of 2017.

I'll always remember spreading his ashes up there on Mount Hood. It took all the strength I had—the second hardest day of my life up to that point. And when I got home, although I could have used a human hug, my black lab Digby was there to greet me, and he made it okay.

The raw truth of it is that my first year of grief was hell. I cried every day, and beyond mere grief, I fell into a state of despair, since my only hope was that it wasn't true, that Brad wasn't really dead. I was fortunate that I was able to take the time off work, and in truth, I barely left the house, spending most of my time in solitude with Digby.

My first grief poem was written the night Brad died, and then I kept on writing. I wrote many poems and letters to him, trying to find words and metaphors for the overwhelming experience of grief that engulfed me. Eventually, I started writing about other things too, like love, philosophy, and nature. Many people will tell you to turn to friends and family to help you through the hardship of grief. But that didn't work for me. I found that the world around me was uncomfortable with my level of distress and ready for me to be better much sooner than I was capable of. So, I found comfort in the quiet nature of my wooded suburban backyard, away from witnessing eyes, and in a place where I could hear my own thoughts. A poem called "Lonesome" I wrote at this early stage of grief captures my state of mind.

Lonesome

Lonesome is the day you died,
And lonesome I shall be.
The only place that lonesome's not,
Is in my memory.

I remember my first time smiling about eight months after Brad's death. My smile came through the joy of watching our dog Digby's excitement over being at a lake. I tossed his ball into the water. He sprang off the dock, dropped into the water with a great splash, retrieved the ball, swam to shore, ran back up the dock, and repeated it over and over again. He had so much pure happiness that even the stone that was my heart smiled that day. That was a breakthrough moment, a turning point. That was the day I sensed that I was going to survive this loss and be okay.

Yet, a year and a half after my husband died, Bevin, one of my best friends, contracted a fatal brain virus. She was the only friend I had whose friendship became stronger after my husband died. Always bubbly and upbeat, Bevin would say things like, "You do grief your way; I love you anyway." She passed away only six weeks from the day we noticed on a walk that something was wrong with her equilibrium. She was forty-two years old. Her death triggered a deep and wounded place inside of me that felt numb with incomprehension. *How and why was this happening to her? And me?*

We often have no choice with many of the difficult social,

emotional, mental, and physical issues we will encounter with grief. Most of us would never suspect how world-altering grief can be. The collateral damage can be vast—losing family and friends, losing faith, losing our health, losing our ability to think clearly, and losing the person we once were. On my grief journey, I felt that I lost my favorite parts of myself, the parts that were happy, with friends and love. It took me a long time to figure out how to adapt to all the changes I was going through. It took overcoming anger and bitterness. It took deep contemplation of big philosophical questions, such as *What is the meaning of life?* or *What is the role of suffering in life?* It took writing poetry. It took my dog Digby.

I think I would not have made it through that time, if not for my dog. Digby saved my life and gave me a reason to care. His playfulness, attentiveness, and loyalty were crucial to my ability to adapt to grief. And more than that, he was the living treasured reminder of my life with Brad. I grew to love Digby with all my heart and soul, and still do, because love never dies.

Six years after Brad died, when Digby was thirteen years old, with a grapefruit sized mass in his lung and cancer on his foot, he passed away. Just like Brad, he died in his bed, with my arms wrapped around him, the back door open, with the cold January air blowing in around us. I still miss him so very much. He was my best friend. Some grief is just so pure that there are no words to capture the feeling. Digby taught me more about love than any living being ever has. He was the best dog in the world, if there ever was one. The day Digby died was the most alone I have ever felt.

Something I know is true—we miss the ones we love when they are gone. This is the heart of grief, for grief is just love with nowhere to go. I wrote a poem after Digby died, and one of the lines has become my signature saying.

*Perhaps, after all, a broken heart is like a broken mirror,
with more places to reflect the light.*

And yet, even sensing the light and love in my heart was a true gift and treasure, it did not stop the pain of losing my beloved dog. The sadness and loneliness were very real. I believe I would have fallen into a bad state of mind, had I not had the mission of scattering his ashes to pull me into action. I knew I needed to get back on my skis to prepare. A wise man, indigenous author and storyteller Martin Prechtel once said something like this: "We can think ourselves into a dark place, but we can't think ourselves out. It takes movement and action to get out of that place, my friend." Another wise man, author, and podcast host Tony Lynch said it this way: "That's right, you're going to have to fight your way out."

And so, I went to the mountains and got back on my skis. I started preparing for and envisioning my trip up to Illumination Rock, that place where I had scattered my late husband Brad's ashes five years prior, where I was planning to bring Digby's ashes. Who would have known that I would have moved halfway across the country, and how big this mission would loom in my heart and mind?

Three months after Digby died, I met a man named Bently on a ski trip. As if an angel had sent him, my prayers were answered by this handsome, sweet, hunky, and fit guy, full of gratitude and Boy Scout's honor. It felt like a fated day, like the kind of day I could turn the corner on my grief and begin again. Indeed, it was—he and I fell in love. He said he'd love me until the day he died. He said we were soulmates, and if he ever lost me, he would find me.

One of our very first conversations centered around the ski

mountaineering trip I was planning to take to Mount Hood to spread Digby's ashes. I explained that it's a journey up steep glaciated slopes to a spectacular viewpoint rock that juts up into the sky, topping out at 9,500 feet. I'd planned on doing the journey alone—a return to that high mountain place where I'd scattered Brad's ashes.

As soon as Bently heard about my mission, he volunteered to join me. There was just one thing he needed to do on the way: visit his best friend, Jim, who was dying of cancer. So, we visited Jim and his wife on the journey west and planned to return to see them again after our trip up to Illumination Rock.

As committed to action as I was, grief wasn't done with me yet. The worst and most traumatic pain was yet to come. The tragic truth of it is that Bently had a blocked artery to his heart that we did not know about. He had a cardiac arrest at high altitude and died up there on that mountain in my arms. He was fifty-three years old.

We were miles up and far away from help. Fortunately, my cell phone worked at that altitude. I phoned 9-1-1, Mountain Rescue, and my mom. And then I wept and wailed as I waited. Bently and I had floated in our bliss for such a short time. It was mind-numbing. Like a strange dream.

Never in a million years did I think... Never could I have imagined the strength it would take coming down from that mountain that we went up together with Digby's ashes. Never could I comprehend that Bently would die in my arms up there. May 20, 2023... the hardest day of my life.

I came down that mountain a different person. I can hardly describe the abyss of trauma and grief I experienced at Bently's sudden death. All the love I had was wrapped up in a knot of pain and loss I didn't know what to do with.

And yet by the time that day was over, amidst the tears and sadness, there was a hardening of my mind, a kind of stoicism setting in. No one was going to rescue me from this mess. I had to be the one to face this night, and the next day, and the rest of my life. I was alone in a sea of pain, and I sensed that I was going to have to fight my way out. "Take it on the chin, stand back up, and take it again" was one of the mantras in my head, one that Bently's best friend Jim used to say. I felt tough as nails and tender as a wilted flower all at the same time. The grief erupted like lava from a spewing volcano, hot and molten, and then hardened into a rock-strewn scorched earth that formed my inner landscape.

But in the end, it wasn't a fight that got me out, but rather, a disciplined mind to accept the suffering and the strength to surrender to the totality of the trauma and grief.

I withdrew into nature and slept in the back of my truck in wild and remote places. For three weeks, I sat by raging rivers and listened to their songs. I lay in my sleeping bag and wept through torrential rain and thunderstorms, my mind raging with disbelief and longing. I made fires and played my guitar to the rhythm of the flames, as my body withered into a shape too thin for my stature. I stared up at star-filled night skies so deep and vast that it made me think profoundly about eternity and the meaning of all of this. I cursed God, frustrated that He thought this was a good plan for my life. I was tormented into half-craziness by dark, anxiety-filled thoughts. Eventually, I made peace with God as I came to understand that He is good, despite all the death, suffering, and evil in this world.

In solitude, I could begin to hear myself think more clearly again. In nature, everything felt simpler. It didn't matter to the trees in the forest or the mountain peaks that I was a woman with a hard story, a broken heart, and apprehension about re-entering the "real world." In nature, my rhythms settled, and my mind started to clear. I noticed small things, such as a spider weaving its web or the sound of a grasshopper moving in the grass.

I remained out in the remote wilderness for about three weeks, which was long enough to gain my equilibrium. And then the call came to be there for Jim, who was now dying. I drove for two days and arrived at dawn to witness a sky the color of a cantaloupe and the Arizona desert blooming in a floral display that comes only once every ten years. Amidst hugs and tears, I was grateful to be there to say goodbye and support Jim in his final days. He passed away on Bently's birthday later that week.

I returned to the mountain shortly after Jim's passing, and despite the icy conditions, I successfully made the solo trip up to Illumination Rock with Digby's ashes. I had rose petals for Bently, a bouquet of flowers for Brad, and love and prayers in my heart.

When I came down off the mountain that day, I felt so lonely, drained, and numb. I felt like I was a paper girl, whose grief-torn heart was scattered like confetti on the mountainside. Eventually, after another few weeks out there surrounded by nature, I left the wild edges of my grief and headed home.

That was two and a half years ago.

In my search for solace, healing, and meaning in the face of my losses, I began writing poems. Over the last seven years, writing poetry gave me a way to take all the fragmented pieces of myself, the amputated hopes and dreams and the pain of a broken heart, and rearrange it all in the kaleidoscope of word art. It became the space where I could begin to see the beauty in my grief and how it helped guide me toward new hopes and dreams for my future. One day, I gathered all my poetry writings in one place and realized there was enough there to fill a book that reflected not just my journey but also my growth through grief and healing. In 2024, I published my first collection of poems called *Illumination - a griever's journey through the darkness.*

I also became a certified grief counselor through the American Academy of Grief Counseling. The journey of becoming a grief counselor began when I struggled to find a grief counselor after Brad died. I left the few sessions I attended feeling as lost and desperate as I was when I started. There were times I felt judged and misunderstood—being told it was my choice to feel better or not. Feeling isolated by this experience, I turned to books and read grief stories by many other people. One of the biggest takeaways from reading these stories was that we must find meaning in our suffering. And when we find the meaning, we can endure.

A small voice inside of me whispered that I had been prepared for this path, and I listened. Taking this step to become a resource for others walking through grief helped me create a framework to begin healing all of the complex experiences and emotions I had endured. I began to realize that my experiences of losing Brad, Digby, Bently and Bevin had given me the heart to offer support to others who are grieving and help them find meaning in their loss.

If grief is the experience we go through when we lose what we love, then mourning is the work we must do to embrace grief into our lives. That work isn't easy; there's no one thing we can do, think, or say that will magically make our pain go away. There's no quick-fix solution. We must allow ourselves to feel all the messy feelings of grief with patience as we begin to unknot the tangle of sadness, anger, guilt, and other feelings that arise within grief.

Research studies have shown that parts of our brain shut down when we experience grief, trauma, and extreme stress in our lives. This can often make us feel numb, confused, and unable to think clearly as we move through grief. When this happens to us, it leads to an inability to speak about our deepest places of pain. This is why music, poetry, and art help us in these moments—they take us out of our brains and allow us to feel the emotions in our hearts and bodies.

The theologian Henri Nouwen once said, "You need to let your wounds go down to your heart. Then you can live through them and discover that they will not destroy you."

When we analyze our wounds through logic and thinking, it's just the beginning of our healing journey. True healing comes when we take our grief into the deepest places within ourselves. And it is from this place that we begin to understand that what we feel we have lost, especially love, can never be destroyed.

I spent a lot of time letting my wounds go down to my heart. The work I'm continuing to do to heal is inside me, hidden in places where no one else can witness. Sitting with the pain of loss and facing its impact on my life in its totality. It's to understand that we carry our lost loved ones inside of us, where they continue to live in our hearts forever.

I also continue to re-engage with activities that bring joy into my life. I am passionate about mountain biking and playing the harp. I have begun to live my life in a more meaningful way by connecting with the community around me rather than isolating myself.

Moving forward through my grief has been a series of choices I've made to live my life through commemoration of the losses I've endured. This can be big things like taking that ski trip I planned with Bently or small things like speaking Brad's name to the evening wind. Commemoration is one way to celebrate our loved ones who have passed on through acts of remembrance.

I've learned many things about life and a deeper understanding of myself through grief.

- I've learned that we can cultivate an unshakeable spirit in the face of suffering and hardship.
- I've learned that we grow the most through times of struggle, not through times of ease.
- I've learned that grief molds us into entirely new people.
- I have learned that love is eternal—it never dies.
- I have learned that we must connect with something, even if it's just nature, or else grief can be very isolating.

So, when does grief begin, and when does it end?

Grief begins with a loss and well… it doesn't end. It remains in us for the rest of our lives. And yet, with time we change how grief resides in us. And eventually we realize that the grief has become something beautiful and valuable, like the love that forged it. And…

Perhaps, after all, a broken heart is like a broken mirror, with more places to reflect the light.

SHALEEM DZON

Shaleem Dzon has been touched by tragedy's blaze more than once. Her book, *Illumination: A Griever's Journey Through the Darkness* (2024), chronicles seven years of grief and renewal through poetry—inspired by a sacred place called Illumination Rock. She's a grief counselor, registered nurse, avid mountain biker, poet, and nature lover. Shaleem is devoted to illuminating the path from sorrow to strength for others walking through loss.

CONNECT WITH SHALEEM HERE

IlluminationGriefCounseling.com

www.empoweredgriefjourney.com/shaleem

Scan to learn more about Shaleem

10

FROM GRIEF TO GRATITUDE

Anda Grobbelaar

O n the first of August 2001, my life changed in a way I could never have imagined. My daughter, Anelda, affectionately called Biebie, was stillborn. I carried Biebie to full term, imagining her cries, her first steps, her laughter filling our home. But instead of welcoming a living child, I was handed a perfectly formed, beautiful, lifeless baby girl who looked like a sleeping doll. Except she would never wake. That day marked the beginning of a journey that would redefine not only my understanding of motherhood and loss but also of purpose, resilience, and spiritual transformation. I didn't know it then, but Biebie's death was the seed of something far greater—a mission to guide others from grief to gratitude.

The weeks following Biebie's stillbirth were some of the most emotionally turbulent of my life. I felt numb and shattered all at once. My body, which had prepared to nourish life, felt like a traitor. My soul, which had dreamed of our family of four, was in mourning. Emotionally, I oscillated between denial, guilt, anger, and overwhelming sadness. There were moments when I couldn't speak, let alone cry. And there were other moments where the tears wouldn't stop.

Having taken time off from my job as a Human Resources Manager for an internal automotive company, I was devastated when the Managing Director phoned me and asked me how I was. All I could say was, "Okay," and he said, "Well you don't sound 'okay.'" What did he expect? I had just lost my baby!

My eldest daughter Lané, only three years old at the time, was furious with me. She called Biebie her "sunflower" and had been waiting so eagerly for her sister's arrival. When I returned home without her, Lané wouldn't let me hold her. That shattered my heart into even smaller pieces.

Physically, I was exhausted. My arms ached to hold the child who would never grow up. My body still carried the instincts of motherhood, but there was no baby to feed or soothe. Spiritually, I felt abandoned. I wrestled with God. I screamed in silence, *Why us? Why me?*

I couldn't understand why something so cruel could happen to someone who had so much love to give.

Yet, amid that darkness, there were lights: My loving husband Len, my ever-present friend Jansie, who dragged me out for tea and shopping, and small rituals that slowly started to breathe life back into me. One of those rituals was simply looking for something beautiful each day: a flower blooming, the changing sky, the sound of birds at dawn. And each morning, we started saying, "Good morning, world," as we opened our blinds in our house with Lané.

No matter the weather, that little act of gratitude reminded us that we were still here, still breathing, still part of life. There were rose trees in my garden, and in the afternoons when Lané came home from playschool we would look at the buds and see how much they had grown since the previous day until they eventually opened. I guess I was trying to teach Lané that there is still life after loss and that it is okay to enjoy something beautiful.

The man who held me together, my husband Len, was my rock. He grieved deeply. Yet every day, he showed up with strength, gentleness, and unwavering love. He held my hand when I couldn't stand. He held our family together when I couldn't function. His love never wavered, even when the grief made us feel distant or short-tempered or confused. Together, we made a promise to each other: We would not be undone by this. And even in our brokenness, we showed up for Lané, for each other, and for the life we were still meant to live. Grief can tear marriages apart. But it can also bind them more deeply. Ours became stronger.

Living in Cape Town, South Africa, where we have such beautiful nature and mountains, Len took me and Lané out on Saturdays and Sundays for lunch or a drive, and all I could see was new moms with their babies. It was so heartbreaking for us, and I would often cry in the restaurant where we were sitting.

One of the most powerful turning points came through the smallest of hands: Lané's. Eventually, she started to warm up to me again. She drew a picture that remains my most cherished keepsake. It shows her understanding: "Daddy put Biebie in Mommy's tummy, but Mommy cries long tears because Biebie is dead. Mommy smiles when Lané comes to Mommy." That innocent insight broke through my emotional wall and reminded me that there was still life here to hold and love.

Another moment of transformation came when I returned to work. It wasn't very easy. People avoided eye contact with me, unsure of what to say. Some offered awkward condolences. Others said nothing at all. The worst was the Managing Director of the company, who bluntly told me I should stay home with my living child, implying that I didn't belong in the working world anymore. His words pierced deeply, but they also ignited something within me: a need to change how society approaches grief. Eventually, I left that position. And honestly, that's when the real journey began.

Over time, my grief gave birth to purpose. I began reading about grief, exploring healing, and understanding that pain can be a portal to purpose. I wrote a book called *Biebie's Story*, not just to honour my daughter but also to help others understand that grief is not a detour in life, it is part of life. When Lané turned eight, she came home one day beaming with excitement and said, "Let's have an angel party for Biebie's birthday!" That first party became a tradition. We donated the gifts Biebie would have received to the children's cancer unit at the Tygerberg Hospital here in Cape Town. Nineteen years later, we still do this every August. Lané's compassion and creativity transformed our loss into light.

My healing didn't happen in a single moment; it happened through small, intentional choices every day. I realised early on that grief is not something to "move on" from, it's something you move forward with. Biebie will always be part of me. Her absence shaped my presence. Her story is intricately woven into who I am. I began to see grief as a spiritual teacher. It taught me patience, compassion, and the importance of being present with others in their pain. I also realised how uncomfortable grief makes people feel, especially when it's not their grief. That discomfort often leads to avoidance or insensitivity, and I wanted to change that.

Writing became a lifeline. Journaling helped me untangle my feelings. Creating rituals of gratitude grounded me. Helping others gave me purpose. I also learned that it's okay to talk about our dead loved ones. Their memory deserves space. You don't just "get over" someone you loved—you learn to live with the void, to love through the ache, and to grow despite the sorrow.

Grief is not linear. It doesn't come with a stopwatch or deadline. It is multi-functional. You can be grieving and laughing in the same breath. You can be in pain and still be grateful. You can cry today and feel joy tomorrow, and both are valid.

Not long after we lost Biebie, God gave us another daughter, Andelé. I often say He must have seen how much we wrestled with Him after Biebie's death, and He responded with a gift wrapped in sunshine. Andelé brought joy, laughter, and a softness that our hearts needed. Lané adored her instantly. Watching them bond was like witnessing a miracle unfold in slow motion. Today, Andelé is her own radiant force. She reminds us that life after loss can still be deeply beautiful. She is the living echo of a healing we never thought possible.

Today, I am a speaker, mentor, and founder of Fire2Wire South Africa, Saudi Arabia, India, and Nigeria; a community born from the teachings of David Nair and the Mental Resilience Mastery (MRM) program that I proudly joined. I help people identify purpose, design their mornings with intention, and understand how energy and mindset shape their lives. Fire2Wire helps people set daily goals, practice affirmations, and build resilience. We teach that your thoughts, emotions, and actions create your reality, and it all starts with awareness.

David challenged me, believed in me, and eventually invited me to become a contributing author to *Grail: Tick Your Life Right with Purpose*. That book was another milestone on this journey. I went from a silently grieving mother to a global storyteller, etching Biebie's story in the lives of people around the world. Through it all, I've stayed grounded in my core values: passion, authenticity, faith, kindness, hope, and love. These values aren't just words—they are the compass that guides my every decision. As Vishen Lakhiani so beautifully put it, "Your life is not about you, but rather your life is about the lives you touch. When you make your life about others, you will never wake up feeling anxious, worried or stressed."

That is my purpose: To help a million people move from grief to gratitude so they no longer feel stuck. So that they understand that loss is not the end of their story, it's the beginning of a new one.

If you are walking through grief right now, I want you to know this: You are not broken. You are not alone. And your pain does not define you. You have every right to mourn. To feel angry. To question. But please don't bury your grief. Let it breathe. Let it speak. Let it teach you. You don't need to move on from your loved one. You move forward with them. Their memory walks beside you. Every step. Every day. Grief is not the opposite of love, it is the continuation of love. Let your tears fall. Let your soul ache. And when you're ready, let your heart open again. Start each day with gratitude. End each night with intention. Write your plans down. Set your priorities. And watch how the universe conspires to support you.

When you feel adrift, remember this: Purpose is your anchor. When you live a life aligned with your soul, things begin to flow. You begin to heal. And when you help others, you heal faster. Biebie's life, though brief, was not in vain. Her story has touched hundreds, and it will touch millions. Through her, I learned to live with open hands, an open heart, and open arms. So today, just for today, decide to be happy with what is yours. Be kind. Be curious. Be present. Laugh freely. Love deeply. Forgive quickly. Because today might just be the most beautiful day of your life.

ANDA GROBBELAAR

Anda Grobbelaar is a transformational coach, speaker, author, and co-founder of Fire2Wire South Africa. With a heart forged through personal loss and resilience, Anda has turned her life's greatest grief, the stillbirth of her daughter Biebie, into a powerful mission: to empower one million individuals to rise from the ashes of grief, burnout, and self-doubt to reclaim their inner fire and live intentional, purpose-driven lives. She is one of the co-authors of *Grail 2.0: Tick Your Life Right with Purpose.*

CONNECT WITH ANDA HERE

https://linktr.ee/anda.grobbelaar
www.empoweredgriefjourney.com/anda

Scan to learn more about Anda

11

GRIEF IS NOT A DETOUR

Aly Bird

The Moment Everything Changed

On the day it happened, I was a three-hour drive away from home with our car. My partner Will and I shared one car because I mostly worked from home or could bike to wherever I needed to go in the small town in western Canada where we lived. November 27, 2019 was an exception. I wanted to hear an author speak in Victoria. So I took our car and traveled the 100 miles down Vancouver Island on my own, leaving my beloved to go on a day hike with a friend.

Sitting in the crowd listening to the author's presentation, I started getting strange phone calls from numbers I didn't recognize. They were from the same area code as mine, so I didn't consider them spam, but I didn't want to miss out on this speaker so I didn't step out to answer them. Finally a number I recognized came up—his aunt, who lived in a time zone three hours ahead of ours. Why would she be calling me at midnight (her time)? Suspicion and anxiety began to rise in my stomach.

When the speaker finished, I found a stairwell and unlocked my phone. I had an eerie sensation in my fingers and toes. I tapped Will's aunt's number in my call history and she picked up on the first ring.

"Oh, Aly. I'm so sorry."

"What's wrong?" My heartbeats grew in strength and reverberated off my rib cage.

"Oh, you don't know? Will—" she choked on her words, "William died."

I remember holding my phone away from my head and lulling my shocked body by repeating the word "no" over and over again until someone found me and asked if I was alright. The answer was simpler than any I had ever given. "No, I'm not okay."

The person I was supposed to spend the rest of my life with was gone. He slipped, he fell, and he got an instantly life-ending head injury. There was no warning. There was no goodbye. I was thirty, alone, and left in a world that no longer made sense to me.

The Shelter of Shock

The early days after my beloved died taught me first-hand how remarkable the human body is at protecting itself. The initial distress of learning that the love of my life was gone and how he'd died lasted no more than forty-eight hours. I wailed. I worried about his body. I curled my body into a ball inside of his North Face hoodie to stay warm in between the sweaty hot flashes of stress that threatened to melt my skin from the inside of my body. Then, I felt almost nothing.

My limbs tingled, but I didn't feel hunger or even a headache develop when surely I was going through caffeine withdrawal. I was dumbfounded by how capable I was at completing tasks without any sleep. Functioning on one to two hours a night, I was choosing urns and caskets, writing eulogies, and fawning over other peoples' pain. Despite the love of my life being gone, I believed I was going to be okay. I was surrounded by people who loved me, who loved him, who loved us. I'd recover from this. I'd make a comeback. And I'd do it fast.

What I know now is that the insomnia would last years. And that initial shock—that protective and desensitizing shock that my brain was offering my body in those early days—made me feel like a fool when it wore off six weeks later.

Now alone, I wasn't left with just heartbreak and longing, I was left in a world that no longer made sense to me anymore and sensations in my body that were foreign, involuntary, and unwelcome. Before my beloved died, I'd never experienced a loss that changed my life so dramatically.

In the world I was familiar with, people died when they were old. If you were a good person, then good things happened to you. I longed for my future because I thought we—me and my beloved, the person I chose to spend my life with—were in control of it. From my spiritual beliefs to my future plans right down to not knowing what possessive pronouns to use, I was left bewildered. Was it still our bed if I would be the only one sleeping in it now?

My World Today

It's been almost six years, and today my grief and I co-exist. I understand it's never going to go away, but I feel like I have more control of the volume dial. I still cry. I still experience new losses because Will isn't here. I still feel rage sometimes. But I don't dismiss my grief. I don't try to ignore it. I don't judge myself when it rises to the surface. Today I believe that grief is worth my time. When my grief asks for my attention, I offer it willingly.

Today, I live around the legacy of Will's life and death. There isn't a part of me or my life that hasn't been touched by it. My forearm is covered in memorial tattoos, including his phone number, which I put there when I finally canceled his phone plan. My dog is named after a song that Will and I used to listen to together. My confidence comes from knowing how much he loved me. My self-compassion was forged in the wake of his death. My bravery comes from knowing that I have survived something horrific and that I am still here.

Today, I'll talk about Will to anyone who'll listen. I don't fear their reaction when I tell stories about a dead man. My friends who knew Will know that he is always welcome in a conversation. They know that even if I cry, it doesn't mean I don't want to talk about him. I even have friends in my social circle who know Will intimately, despite never meeting him.

Today, I'm a therapist. I work with young adults who have been traumatically bereaved. I sit with them and listen to their pain and their fears, and I witness the many ways that their grief manifests in their lives from moment to moment. I ask them to tell me everything about what they're experiencing and about their person who died. I tell each of them that their grief does not and will not scare me. And I love my job.

The Road Without a Map

I can't tell you every step in the process of how I've survived in this world without Will. Even if I did, one of the many things that suck about grief is that it's different for everyone. I can't give you a roadmap, even though I know you want one.

What I can offer you is a few things that have helped me. These concepts have made my pain easier to manage, even if only a little, and a path forward easier to find. Please take what is useful and leave the rest.

1) Treat everything as an experiment now.

After the person you love most in the world dies, everything you do becomes an experiment. Every action—big or small—is a test of what fits now. Getting out of the house, touching their belongings, attending a social event, watching a show you used to love: none of it comes with a clear answer. So treat each thing as an experiment. Try it. See how it feels in this version of your life. If it feels too hard, too soon, or just wrong—you're allowed to stop, say no, or try something different. That's not failure. That's wisdom. On the other hand, if something brings a tiny flicker of ease, comfort, or aliveness—notice that. Follow it. Let it guide you forward. Your grief will evolve, and your capacity will shift, so what doesn't work today might feel better in a week, a month, or a year. You're allowed to reassess at any time. You can change your mind. You don't need to push through to prove anything. The most important thing is to listen to yourself. You have agency here. Let this be the beginning of trusting yourself again in a world that now feels upside down.

2) Make things easier and more comfortable.

Grief can't be fixed—but that doesn't mean you're powerless. You can't undo the loss, but you can make choices that bring a little more ease and a little more comfort to your day. Start small. Wear soft, comfortable clothes. Eat what's easy. Rest when you're tired. Let go of the pressure to function like you used to. You have permission to lower your expectations of what you can accomplish right now and for however long you need to. That might mean asking for a lighter workload or taking longer to respond to emails. It might mean stepping back from family conversations that feel too charged or setting limits on how much caretaking or decision-making you're able to do. You might decline social invitations, leave early, or ask a friend to just come sit quietly with you. These aren't failures—they're wise, protective choices. Grief takes up space. Let your care for yourself take up space, too. You won't be able to fix your grief, but you will need to survive. Anything that helps you do that—anything that brings even a little bit of relief—is worth choosing.

3) Offer a little feedback or guidance.

The people who love you unconditionally want to help you—but they may not know how. Grief changes your needs, your boundaries, your energy, and your capacity—and the people closest to you can't guess what that looks like unless you tell them. Offering feedback, even if it feels a little uncomfortable, can make living with your grief and without the person who died just a little easier. Let your people know what helps and what doesn't. Tell them if a certain phrase shuts you down, if their silence feels supportive or isolating, or if you need more check-ins—or fewer.

Say, "Can you just sit with me instead of trying to cheer me up?" or "It helps when you text before you call."

Offering a little guidance or feedback isn't being demanding—it's helping the people who already love you to love you better. You deserve care that actually fits what you need, and the people who are truly in your corner want to give you the care you need. Give them the chance to do that.

4) Trust the wisdom of your body.

Grief doesn't just happen in your thoughts—it happens in your body. In Western culture, we're taught to push through pain, to rely on logic, to think our way out of discomfort. But grief isn't something you can outsmart. It's a full-body experience that arrives uninvited and unfolds without your control. You may feel exhausted, foggy, tense, nauseated, restless, numb—these are not signs of weakness. They're signs that your body is responding to profound loss. Instead of judging yourself or trying to push past your limits, try listening.

Your body is not the enemy—it's on your team. It's doing its best to protect you, to hold what your mind alone can't carry. If you're tired, rest. If you feel the need to move, walk. If your appetite is off, be gentle with how and what you eat. Respect what your body is asking for. Trust that it knows what it's doing, even when you don't understand it. That trust is not just survival—it's self-compassion.

5) Understand that you are not broken.

You are human. Grief is one of the most deeply human experiences we have—and yet in the modern world, we've done a poor job of honoring it. We're expected to bounce back, stay productive, and return to who we were before, as if grief is just a disruption instead of a transformation. You are not a failure if you don't feel like the same person you were when your person was alive. Of course you're different—someone is missing from your life.

Grief reshapes your priorities, your energy, your identity, your relationships. And in that reshaping, you don't have to leave your person in the past. The version of you that's emerging gets to carry their memory, their influence, their love—whether it's visible to others or just something you hold quietly inside. This isn't dysfunction; it's your humanity responding to loss.

Give yourself permission to change. You're not meant to "get back to normal"—you're meant to find your way forward, and your person can still be a part of that. There's nothing broken about you. You're doing the very human work of living with loss.

Grief is Not a Detour

In the beginning, I didn't know how I would survive. I couldn't imagine a version of life without Will that didn't feel unbearable. I thought I had to outrun my grief. I thought I'd be able to overcome it with logic and relentless action. I didn't yet understand that grief would become a part of me—not something to get through, but something that I just live with. Now, I know better.

Grief doesn't go away, but it does change its shape. It softens in some places and deepens in others. It has helped me to be present to joy, connection, and even laughter. It has taught me how to be more human, how to live with more presence and compassion—for myself and for others.

If you're early in your grief, you don't need to know how this ends. You only need to stay close to what is true for you today. Trust your body. Offer feedback to the people who love you. Let yourself rest. You are not failing because you are hurting. You are not broken because you are different now. Grief is not a detour from your life; it's part of the journey. My hope for you is that the road you are on can still lead you somewhere meaningful.

ALY BIRD

Aly Bird is a grief and trauma therapist who works with individuals, couples, and teens navigating life-changing losses and diagnoses. After enduring a life-altering loss herself, she pursued advanced degrees and specialized training to support others through their own grief with compassion, insight, and skill. She is also the author of *Grief Ally: Helping People You Love Cope with Death, Loss, and Grief*, a practical and heartfelt guide for those supporting someone through grief.

CONNECT WITH ALY HERE

www.alybird.com
www.empoweredgriefjourney.com/aly

Scan to learn more about Aly

12

THE ABUSIVE FATHER WHO NEVER CAME BACK

Russell Tellup

I was five years old. I didn't move fast enough when my father wanted me to. He picked me up off the living room floor, slammed my body into the hallway walls as he carried me to my room, kicked the door open, and threw me inside. All through my childhood, moments like this taught me to disappear. To stay small. To read every room like a war zone. And eventually, to abandon myself to survive.

My father died around 2020 from COVID. We hadn't spoken in over 25 years. He was an evil, psychotic, narcissistic man. Abusive in every way. The world felt safer to me without him in it. At first, after I learned of his death, I felt free. Free to be me in ways I had never allowed myself to be. Free to speak in ways I hadn't spoken before because his cruel teachings had always echoed inside my mind. I didn't grieve. His death barely came up in conversation. Maybe once or twice with my brother, casually. There was no sadness, no weight of loss. Just relief. Just open space.

But about a year later, while I was watching a stand-up comedy special, something hit me sideways. The comedian was talking about his estranged father. How the man came back after his son found success. How the comedian agreed to meet him at a restaurant. How he sat across from his father and let it all out: the pain, the abandonment, the damage.

I started crying. Not because I lost my dad. Not because I missed him. I cried because I would never get that dinner. I would never have the chance to look him in the eyes and tell him what he did to me. What he did to us. I would never get to hear him say, "I'm sorry."

My grief wasn't about loss. It was about the absence of resolution. The stolen opportunity for closure. The confrontation that would never happen. That was when the weight landed.

That moment cracked something open in me. For the first time, I saw myself as someone who had been hurt. Who had endured. And who deserved to heal. That moment quietly launched my healing journey.

Shortly afterward, I tried Rapid Transformational Therapy (RTT). I had no idea what I know now as a trauma-informed somatic coach. No real framework. Just a feeling that something needed to change. RTT works at a subconscious level to reprogram beliefs in order to change behaviors. It's a combination of cognitive behavioral therapy (CBT), hypnosis, and neuro-linguistic programming (NLP). It allows access to deeply rooted belief systems that often drive our choices, habits, and emotional responses—especially those formed in early childhood.

In one session, I remembered something from childhood. I had forgotten to take the trash out. I was asleep. My father came in and dumped the trash all over me while I slept.

I didn't understand the meaning then, but my body did. Why was I always on edge? Why did I always feel threatened, like I was waiting for a blow?

That memory gave me the first clue: I was living in a perpetual trauma response. My body wasn't just stuck in fear. It was trapped in survival mode.

The traumatic moments I had experienced all through my childhood—like that, and so many others—taught me something dangerous and invisible: that I was not enough. That I would never be enough. That nothing I said or did would ever be right. That I was unlovable.

That conditioning seeped into my nervous system, wiring me for chronic survival mode and a desperate, aching need for validation from others. My self-worth was outsourced. My sense of identity was built around proving my value to those people who withheld their approval.

Naturally, I was drawn to narcissistic relationships in adulthood. Familiar dynamics. Power imbalances. Conditional affection. The abuse repeated itself with new faces, and each time, it reinforced the original lie: I was unworthy.

I grew up in southern Ohio. My mother stayed with my father until I was about five years old. She finally left him, and we moved to Colorado. For a short time, it felt like maybe life could be different. But soon afterward, we went back to Ohio for what was supposed to be a vacation—and we were kept there, not sent back to Colorado. By the time I was seven or eight, I ended up living with my father full-time. That's when the abuse really escalated.

My brother Tom and I leaned on each other to survive. We were told over and over by our father that we were the only people in the world we could trust. Everyone else was the enemy. That kind of conditioning sunk deep, but it also bound us together. We became each other's lifelines. That closeness carried into adulthood—we still share everything, even working in the same trade to this day.

As I got older, the survival strategies of childhood became the struggles of adulthood. I had no template for healthy connection. I stumbled in friendships and sabotaged romantic relationships. I struggled with sex addiction and addictive personality traits that kept me constantly restless, chasing intensity instead of intimacy. I was always the loudest, most vulgar, most shocking person in the room—desperate for attention but unable to receive love as safety. Anything good that came into my life, I tore apart before it could stay. I didn't know how to hold it. I wasn't wired for it.

Another turning point came during a breathwork session, about a year later. I was lying on the floor, breathing deeply in a hyperventilation pattern. My body began to seize. My joints curled in. My arms locked tight into the fetal position. It felt like something was about to break. My whole system was on high alert.

Breathwork, specifically somatic breathwork, uses patterned breathing to bypass the thinking mind and tap into the body's emotional memory. It can trigger cathartic releases, mystical experiences, or even bring up novel insights. In some cases, it quiets the brain's default mode network—the same part that psychedelic drugs deactivate—which allows healing to surface in unexpected, profound ways.

Then the breathwork coach asked, "Was it someone at school? Was it your mother? Was it your father?" As soon as she said, "Was it your father?" my entire body went limp. And I cried. Deep, primal sobs. I cried like a baby.

At that moment, I had a vision: I walked into the room and picked myself up off the couch. I held me. The infant version of me. Comforted him. I was both people at once. It might sound strange, but it was real. A full-body, full-heart release.

And then another memory returned. I was three days old. First day home from the hospital. Lying on the couch next to my father. I cried. He picked me up. And he spanked me. That's not a memory I recalled myself—a family member told me that story.

The meaning came later. That moment of picking up my infant self was a re-parenting. A deep cellular reminder that I could give myself the safety I had always longed for. Healing doesn't come from the mind alone—it comes from the body. From compassion. From holding space for the pain. From being willing to feel it, cry it, breathe through it, and witness it without shame. I learned that the threat I was always responding to didn't exist in the present. It was a nervous system imprint. A somatic memory of years lived in fear.

And that child inside me? He still needed someone. So I became that someone. Not overnight. Not all at once. But breath-by-breath. Moment-by-moment. I practiced being safe in my own body. I used tools: breathwork, somatic resourcing, brainspotting, parts work. Not to fix myself, but to meet myself. I do a lot of self-hypnosis. Self-brainspotting. Meditation. Journaling. These are the ways I return to myself. I've learned that I am my source of comfort. I am my source of strength. I am the one who can make sure that I feel safe and loved. As I began to heal, I started using specific tools that rewired the survival patterns my body had learned.

Here's a short explanation of each tool:

- **Somatic resourcing** is about finding safety in the body. It can be as simple as noticing your breath, feeling your feet on the floor, or placing a hand on your chest to anchor yourself. These practices teach the nervous system that the present moment is different from the past.

- **Brainspotting** works by focusing the eyes on specific points in space, which link to stored emotional experiences in the brain. When your gaze lands in those spots, the body often begins processing trauma that words alone can't reach. It's a gentle but profound way to let the nervous system release what it has held for decades.

- **Parts work** is about recognizing that we all have different aspects of ourselves—protectors, inner children, managers—that show up to keep us safe. Instead of fighting those parts, we listen to them with compassion, building trust so they no longer have to run our lives from the shadows.

These approaches helped me stop abandoning myself. They gave me ways to notice when I was slipping into fight, flight, freeze, or fawn mode—and to come back to safety, breath-by-breath.

I still carry emotional scars. I still get triggered. But I don't abandon myself anymore. I no longer live under the influence of a man who hasn't touched me in decades. I've learned to speak without fear of his voice in my head. I've learned that silence is not safety. I've learned that grief is not always about missing someone. Sometimes it's about mourning what never was.

It feels strange to grieve someone who caused so much harm. But I'm not grieving my father's death. I'm grieving the impossibility of reconciliation. The closure that will never come. I'll never get to sit across from him and say, "What you did was wrong. It hurt." And hear him say the words, "I'm sorry." But I've made peace with the fact that I'll never get an apology. Because I no longer need one.

Now I help others find that kind of peace. I work with clients who've lived through similar patterns. I co-regulate with them, hold space for them. Because when we can't co-regulate with an adult as children, we get stuck in trauma loops.

And healing requires being witnessed. It requires someone who can sit with you, emotionally regulated, while you fall apart. That's what I can do now—because I've done it for myself first. That's what all of this gave me: the ability to show up authentically and grounded. To down-regulate my clients not just with words, but with presence.

If you're reading this, there's a good chance you've been carrying difficult things for a long time. Maybe you've convinced yourself it wasn't that bad. Maybe you've been waiting for someone to validate it. To say, "Yes, that was real. That shouldn't have happened."

You don't need anyone else to confirm it. You already know. Your body knows. Your tears know. The tension, the shutdowns, the fear. They know.

Grief isn't linear. Healing isn't pretty. Some days you might feel strong. Other days, you might feel like a scared kid just trying to breathe. That's okay. The most important thing is this: stop abandoning yourself. Start showing up. Start listening. Start being the one who stays.

There is a version of you who isn't afraid anymore. Who isn't living under anyone else's rules. Who trusts their body. Who speaks their truth. And that version is waiting. Right on the other side of your willingness to feel.

You don't have to do it all today. Just keep showing up. One breath at a time.

RUSSELL TELLUP

Russell Tellup is a trauma-informed somatic coach, brainspotting practitioner, and hypnotherapist. He works with survivors of complex trauma, nervous system shutdown, trauma bonds, and toxic relational patterns—especially those who learned to smile while disappearing. His approach is direct, body-based, and compassion-led.

CONNECT WITH RUSSELL HERE

https://russtellup.thementalwellbeingcompany.com

www.empoweredgriefjourney.com/russ

Scan to learn more about Russell

13

CULTIVATING MEANING AFTER LOSS

Gabriella Richardson

I remember it vividly: the imprint of my wet swimsuit on my uncle Kevin "KC's" shirt as I hugged him at my fourteenth birthday party. I had no way of knowing this was the last time I would hug him. Less than two weeks later, my grandmother found him after he had taken his own life. Eight months later, my grandfather passed away from complications related to Parkinson's disease. Two months after that, my great-grandmother died as I was on my way to see her. When I was fifteen, my father chose to leave my life, acting as though he never knew me.

My mother's side of the family was small and tightly bonded. Despite how large and widely dispersed Las Vegas, Nevada was, we chose to live within a few miles of each other. Most Sundays, we would spend time enjoying a meal together, and we'd never dream of spending holidays with anyone else. Within one year, our family had lost half its members. And just like that, it was my mother, my grandmother, and myself. We were inseparable.

The Beliefs That Grief Built

During a time when I was already wrestling with identity, self-worth, and teenage turbulence, my world was flipped inside out. The false sense of stability I held on to in those around me seemed to evaporate, leaving me feeling lost. I remember thinking that family would always be there despite the challenges life brought. How could I make sense of this at such a pivotal age? There was no making sense of any of it—especially Uncle KC's death. Losing him was the hardest.

KC was one of the most accepting, loving, and goofy figures in my life. How could I not feel so close to him? Because my own father did not accept me for who I was, I naturally bonded with Uncle KC, who celebrated and appreciated me. A "gentle giant" at 6' 10", he rode a Harley-Davidson motorcycle, wore full sleeves of tattoos, had no hair on his head but proudly presented a pristine handlebar mustache, and was the kindest, gentlest, silliest person I ever knew. He collected Hot Wheels, Beanie Babies, coins, and many other things, all within his hand-painted pink house. Then he was suddenly gone, leaving behind unanswered questions.

Watching my grandmother grapple with PTSD from discovering her son's body and seeing my mother mourn her oldest brother, I internalized a core belief: My pain is less significant than theirs. I have to be strong for them.

I remember helping clean out Uncle KC's home the day he died. As my mother and I carefully packed up his collection of miniature Caterpillar "Earth Mover" figurines, we noticed a small area of dried blood missed by the cleaning crew. I insisted on being the one to clean up the blood—a symbolic act that anchored my newly formed belief: *Other people's emotions matter more than mine. I must be strong for them. I need to clean this up.*

Yes, I literally cleaned it up. I pretended to be unaffected while attempting to shield my mom and grandmother from this tragedy. I immediately made myself out to be stoic and independent. The suppression of the grief and all other emotions was what I thought would help me move through the trauma I was immersed in. That was the moment I chose to no longer be a child.

The Cost of Suppressed Grief

At the time, I was already a high-achieving high school student in Advanced Placement classes, involved in community service, and committed to building a flawless college résumé. My rebellion was mild: heavy metal music and outfits designed to mortify my sweet, proper mother. Regardless, I still earned good grades and avoided trouble.

The human brain fascinated me. I couldn't understand how the same squishy ball of neurons could lead one person to be a prominent, vibrantly healthy, and successful humanitarian, another to develop Parkinson's, and another—my dearest uncle—to die by suicide. So, I did all the "right" things, seeking acceptance from others, starting with attending college and earning a degree in neuroscience. I moved to Colorado, married my high school sweetheart, bought a modest house in a suburb of Denver, and worked as the Activities Director at a senior living community nearby.

But the truth was, I was deeply unhappy. Even the mention of suicide in a movie or a song would send me into a panic. In my twenties, I clung to KC's photos and figurines with desperation. The belief that I didn't matter as much as others still ruled my life. I was miserable in my marriage, always putting other people's comfort before my own peace, and I couldn't stand being alone with my thoughts. I experienced regular panic attacks, worried that anyone would abandon me at any given time, and desperately clung to the unhealthy dynamic my then-husband and I created.

My mind was a relentless tormentor.
I didn't believe that I deserved a better life.
I didn't believe I was deserving, worthy, or enough.

As a result, I was unhealthy, inactive, overweight, inflamed, and my body hurt. The source of my agony was a mystery at the time, leaving me feeling defeated. I often would say to myself, *I made this bed; now I must lay in it.*

A Turning Point

After ending my first marriage, I reclaimed the pieces of myself that I thought would heal me. I got my first tattoo in memory of my Uncle KC and began dancing again—a hobby I had lost touch with over the years. Following a dance class, I met DJ, the man I am now happily married to. Early in our relationship, I cried to him and exclaimed, "I do not deserve this!" when he offered me a simple compliment. At that moment, I realized I needed to begin therapy immediately. To my surprise, I came to understand just how tightly Uncle KC's suicide had gripped my life. I worked to lessen my physical trauma response through Eye Movement Desensitization and Reprocessing (EMDR), a type of psychotherapy used to support

PTSD treatment. The sessions helped me finally desensitize to the pain stemming from the losses I experienced as a teenager.

EMDR therapy gave me the ability to recount traumatic events in my life without being sent into a panic attack. I could finally talk about Uncle KC's suicide and about the emotional abuse in my previous marriage. While I could recount the events, the abandonment trauma was still so powerful that I had begun taking a low dose of a mood-stabilizer to support my continued healing journey. The logic was that if I could remain stabilized, I would be more effective in therapy and move through my healing journey more efficiently.

Later, DJ and I began a journey of therapy and personal development together. I started to see the belief and behavior patterns that had been running on autopilot in my life—especially the deeply ingrained story of "I'm not enough." I began the work of dismantling it because these were the roots of what had been negatively affecting my beliefs and behaviors.

In my teens and early twenties, I thought strength meant shoving the pain into a box deep in my subconscious and allowing it to collect dust, as if my mind and my body would forget. I learned the real strength is in patiently and compassionately exploring and unraveling the contents of those dusty old boxes.

Everything is Subjective

One of the more controversial and fascinating nuggets of wisdom I've gained in my life is this: events are meaningless. If your initial reaction is anything like mine when I first heard that statement, you might already be considering skipping ahead, and I get it. But hear me out.

With an open mind, imagine you are at an outdoor wedding

ceremony and it starts raining. Water droplets falling from the sky due to atmospheric conditions is simply a physical event with no inherent meaning. Here are some different interpretations, or stories, that may be created as a result of the rain. The bride may say, "This is terrible—the rain ruined the perfect day I've planned for years. I clearly don't deserve nice things." The grandparents may say, "Rain on a wedding day is good luck; it means a strong, lasting marriage." The photographer may say, "Great! Rain adds a cinematic touch to the photos." A disgruntled guest may say, "This wedding was a disaster."

The event of rain during a wedding ceremony holds no inherent meaning. The meaning is in the interpretation that we give events we experience, and that interpretation can shape how we decide to move forward.

So how does this connect with my story so far? The meanings I attached to experiencing death and loss at a young age profoundly influenced the path I took through life and the beliefs I built about myself. I developed the belief that my feelings did not matter as much as my mother's or grandmother's. There were people I spoke with who said suicide is the most selfish thing a person can do and it is not worth grieving their loss. Plenty of people shared their opinions on how I should or should not grieve, based on what they thought was most effective. I am the one who decided that my mother's and grandmother's pain was more significant than my own and suppressed my emotions as a result.

Choosing Differently

When I was in my late twenties, my grandmother was diagnosed with Alzheimer's disease, which she lived with for several years. Though I lived in Colorado, I would regularly fly back to spend extended periods in Nevada helping care for her while my mom took breaks from primary caregiving. In my grandma's final days, we moved her into my mother's spare bedroom for hospice care. When the nurse told my mother and me that Grandma had approximately one month left, I made plans to return after a week in Colorado to be with her when the time came.

A few days later, I was at the gym when my mom called to let me know that my grandmother only had a couple days left. I scrambled to find the earliest flight from Colorado to Nevada. A major snowstorm was coming, threatening to ground flights. Should I drive? Should I try to beat the storm? Was it worth sacrificing safety and the progress my husband and I were making after a recent separation? I paused the panic, and I thought of my grandmother. I called my mom back. "Maybe I should stick with my original flight," I said. "I'd rather spend New Year's Eve with DJ, rebuilding our relationship, than risk being stranded in an airport with strangers. And let's be honest—if grandma knew I chose to watch her die instead of work to repair my relationship, she would haunt me for the rest of my days." My mom agreed, and we laughed. I hung up the phone. Then it rang. My grandmother had just passed away.

I immediately called DJ to tell him my Grandma had passed moments ago and that I would be home from the gym in a few minutes. I walked in the door to see him packing my suitcase so I could catch the next flight to Las Vegas. The flight options loaded on his computer while he threw the most absurd combination of clothes and underwear into a bag for me. He embraced me as I sobbed into his shoulder. My throat was tight. I felt conflicted by the grief of loss and the loving warmth that he knew me so well that he assumed my first thought was to go. While I appreciated the effort from DJ to help me get to see my family as soon as possible, I was still committing to my previous plan. I stayed in Colorado to welcome the New Year.

Peace in the Decision

I wasn't shocked to learn my grandma had passed earlier than estimated. I didn't feel overwhelmed by grief. Instead, I felt a sense of wonder at the synchronicity of it all. Flights were grounded by the storm that evening, and I spent New Year's Eve with my husband, taking a step toward healing. That night, I wore a matching set of earrings and necklace that were my Grandma's and found myself gently touching them through the night as I thought of her.

That decision to stay in Colorado on New Year's Eve marked one of the first times I truly chose myself. Not out of selfishness but a moment of deep clarity. This moment was exactly what I needed to move forward in the new life I was building. I didn't need to be there for the exact moment of her passing to prove my love. She knew what she meant to me, and I finally learned that I don't have to abandon myself in order to honor others.

This left a stillness in my heart. I grieved, but it felt lighter this time. I simply miss having her around. Instead of spiraling into a panic, I fondly think of my Grandma every time I make pancakes—reminiscing about her teaching me the exact moment to flip a pancake when I was far too young to be standing on a stool next to her at the stove. I am filled with love each time I remember this strong woman who helped raise me.

What Now?

The thought of living a happy life seemed so far out of reach for me. The past version of myself would never have imagined a future self who is typing this story to have become so empowered, free, happily married, resilient, healthy, and strong. My last panic attack was before I got pregnant with my two-year-old daughter. I haven't taken medication for almost three years now. I started lifting weights consistently and have lost over fifty pounds, feeling healthier than ever. I sleep well, and my body feels at peace. I no longer feel a constant tightness in my chest, the chronic pain and inflammation are gone, and I can easily slow the thoughts in my mind through meditation. My life is fulfilling now, and each day is filled with purpose.

I am so grateful and proud of who I am continuing to become—no longer bound by the scars of my past traumas of Uncle KC's suicide, my father's abuse and absence from my life, a difficult divorce, and the passing of my beloved grandmother.

If you're finding yourself healing from grief, seeking transformation, or longing for stillness in your soul, that future absolutely exists, and it is full of hope. My story is no fairy tale, though. Therapy and a series of fantastic personal development classes didn't magically "cure" me. I didn't walk away from grief and self-sacrifice into a rainbow-filled life. The old stories I built as a teenager still run in the background, ready to take over if I'm not careful. I made a conscious effort to rewrite my story and you can, too. It takes vigilance and intention to live differently.

Today, I've chosen a career path where I help other people uncover and shift their own belief systems. I work in the personal development industry offering coaching to individuals, leading workshops and corporate trainings, and developing programs to support individual healing. Through my podcast, *Nexus of Narratives,*

I reach further into my purpose by facilitating compassionate conversations to bridge differences in belief systems. Guiding someone to an "aha" moment about themselves is magic; it feels like exactly where I'm meant to be.

A Final Thought

Imagine your mind as a perfectly tilled plot of land at birth, ready for seeds to be planted. Some seeds we planted ourselves. Others blew in from nearby fields or were transported by wildlife. What grows depends on what was planted and how the land was tended—in other words, what conditions cultivated the growth of these seeds. Now, as adults, we can look at our internal landscapes and ask, *Are these beliefs still serving me?* If not, we have to do the hard work of pulling weeds, tracing their roots, and cultivating something new. You, me, all of us—we're not broken. We just need to do a little gardening.

GABRIELLA RICHARDSON

Gabriella Richardson is a dynamic coach, consultant, and community leader who brings together intellect, empathy, and purpose-driven strategy to create lasting impact. As the founder of *The Nexus Impact* and host of the *Nexus of Narratives* podcast, she specializes in blending data-informed insight with the power of personal storytelling to drive meaningful transformation. With a background in neuroscience and a career in personal development, Gabriella supports uncovering belief systems and building conscious leadership to foster measurable growth.

CONNECT WITH GABRIELLA HERE

www.thenexusimpact.com
www.empoweredgriefjourney.com/gabriella

Scan to learn more about Gabriella

14

ASHES INTO GOLD
AN ALCHEMY OF ANGER AND GRIEF
Talya Pardo Ricardo

Inherited Fire

Anger was the main emotion expressed in my family growing up. My father would explode, and my mother would defend herself by matching his energy and yelling back. My brother and I learned to stay quiet, bracing for what might come next. When the shouting stopped, silence took its place. But nothing would happen. I struggled to make sense of the pain. There were never any attempts to resolve these anger-fueled outbursts, no caring apology, and no conversation to work through the disagreements. We could feel the resentment vibrating off our parents from the tension that lingered heavily in the air.

My parents taught me from an early age that explosive anger and resentment were how to communicate and express myself. I was never given the tools or shown how to communicate in a healthy way the deeper emotions I hid underneath the surface: my sadness, fear, and disappointment. Not knowing any better, I was carrying these patterns of communication forward into every relationship believing this was normal. I was given the nickname "fiery" by those around me and wore this title like a protective badge of armor.

The Breaking Point

The fire within me continued to burn unchecked for fourteen years of marriage. I lived in a constant state of volatility and instability, meeting my husband's anger with my own. Each of us being fueled by old wounds and unhealed trauma. Each time I thought I was standing up for myself in our arguments, I was carrying forward the old familiar patterns from my childhood that I knew all too well. I was living out my parents' relationship of repeated conflict that perpetuated anger and resentment.

Our problems continued to grow when my husband was injured during a work accident, where he lost the use of his left arm and developed a rare, severe pain condition. I quickly became a caretaker to my husband, helping him dress, preparing his food, and accompanying him to endless hospital visits. It was challenging for him to be present in our relationship and family because of the prescription medications he was taking to manage his pain. At the same time, I was taking care of our two little girls and working a full-time job to keep us afloat.

I was overwhelmed and exhausted having to support the entire household alone. I had become, all at once, a single mother, caretaker, and sole provider. I was thrown into survival mode, with no emotional capacity or ability to cope with our new reality. Our fights began to erupt more often and were followed by long, icy silence. My anger reached new heights as I lashed out at everyone around me, including the ones I loved most, my children.

I yelled.

I screamed.

I raged.

I overreacted.

My life began to feel like a song playing on repeat, over and over again. I would get angry, then promise myself it wouldn't happen again, but it always did. Remorse followed me like a shadow I didn't want to acknowledge, yet it was always there. I was trapped in a loop I didn't know how to break.

The Mirror Moment

My turning point with anger happened when my oldest daughter was seven. I yelled at her—about what, I can't even remember. But this time, she yelled back. It was like looking into a mirror and seeing my angry self reflected right in front of me. In that moment, reality clicked: *Oh my goodness! She gets that from me!*

The shock of that realization hit hard. I saw, for the first time, how deeply my anger was affecting my children. I suddenly became overtaken with guilt and shame. I realized I was carrying the same generational pattern from my own childhood into my family.

After moments like this, I would tell my girls, "Mommy won't yell like that again," and see the hurt in their eyes wash over them. Their hesitation and withdrawal were palpable when I calmed down and slipped into the guilt phase of my anger. I often pulled away from them, unable to face the pain I had caused.

I had betrayed the most sacred contract between a mother and her children: to protect, nurture, and guide them with love. I was supposed to be their rock, their safe space. They needed me to have the emotional capacity to teach them compassion and patience, especially amid the stress of custody changes with their father. The realization that I had not been that sanctuary to them hit me like a punch to the gut.

My exhaustion, overwhelm, and lack of self-awareness weren't their fault, yet they bore the weight of it. They went to school carrying my impatience when they bickered instead of getting ready. They went to bed with sadness after I snapped at them to stop complaining and go to sleep.

I was ashamed of the mother I had been. Ashamed of losing control when frustration turned to anger. The weight of it pressed on my heart and shoulders, dragging my self-esteem into a spiral of self-blame. The realization of how my anger had shaped their childhood made me feel like I had failed at the most important role I'd ever been given. I feared I had become the source of their lifelong pain, just as my parents had been for me.

This was my awakening. The denial shattered. I knew I had to change, not just for them, but for myself. I realized that anger wasn't who I was. It was a language I had learned, and one I could finally unlearn.

The Turning Point

My healing journey began two years after finalizing my divorce through a series of small awakenings and quiet insights. New experiences opened my eyes to help me feel empowered as I stepped into what I now call my *Queen Energy*. For the first time in my life, I could hold my head high and see strength where I once saw only failure. I was finally starting to see the real version of myself that had been hiding behind anger all these years.

At first, I thought my search for healing was about recovering from my marriage and the trauma I had endured. But beneath the surface pain was something much deeper within me. The anger I had inherited from my family and was passing on to my own. I began to see how childhood patterns had followed me into motherhood. My temper, my yelling, the harsh words. I was repeating history. My daughters were living the same fear I had once known.

This realization became the true purpose of my healing: to break the generational cycle that was bestowed upon me. My desire was strong to heal the anger from my childhood so I could become the mother my daughters needed me to be. As my awareness deepened, I could see the pain my short temper had caused. The words I used echoed my mother's voice when I was young.

The pain of my anger had become unbearable. I sought help from mentors, counselors, and therapists who began to uncover the "why" behind my anger. It was through the most vital step of radical self-acceptance that I was finally able to release the ego that kept me righteous and learn humility. I began to take full responsibility for my behavior, the words, the tone, the explosions, and face what they had cost me.

I began to learn that anger is both a messenger and a mirror. It points to deeper wounds, unmet needs, and beliefs about our self-worth. Healing from anger is similar to learning a new language. It took time to learn how to express my anger in a healthy way by finding new words for my feelings and connecting differently with the sensations in my body that arose within seconds of being triggered. By tuning into my body, I was able to become more aware of my anger and allowed myself to take time to process what was happening before reacting with anger. One way that I did this was through learning how to breathe—literally.

The first real tool I began using in moments of anger was exaggerated, deep breathing. When I would feel my anger begin to rise within me, I would stop and take long, loud breaths in and out. It was so dramatic that my girls would giggle and say, "Mommy's ha-ing again!" Their laughter broke the tension every time. It wasn't perfect, but it worked. Each deep breath gave me a few precious seconds to choose differently—to respond instead of react. This was the beginning of a new chapter with my children. One where they could feel safe around me and where I could become the mother I needed to be for them.

As I continued to practice small shifts like deep breathing, something beautiful happened. I began to give myself grace. I stopped expecting perfection and started accepting progress. On days where it was hard to manage my anger, I started to ask myself, *What can I learn from this moment?* This question became a lifeline in these moments as it allowed me to reflect instead of spiraling into my old patterns of shame, guilt, and blame. It was about returning to love faster each time than I had previously.

One of the greatest gifts of my healing journey was realizing that the black hole of guilt and shame wasn't the full truth. Beneath it, there was still love, effort, and goodness. Breathing deeply, giving myself grace, and practicing self-compassion allowed me to see that I wasn't a terrible mother. I was a human one, learning to do better.

The Alchemy of Healing

The anger didn't go away overnight, but this was a start. I

began to celebrate my small wins—every time I breathed instead of yelled, every moment I apologized instead of defended. Slowly, the explosions became fewer and softer. I learned to own my actions and talk through them afterward, and those moments became the foundation for my healing. Through self-compassion and grace, I've learned to accept myself fully, flaws and all. Healing doesn't happen by punishing ourselves for our mistakes; it begins when we understand why we made them and choose differently the next time. Every breath, every apology, every act of self-compassion is an alchemical step, turning ashes into gold. I can't change the past, but I can shape the present, and in doing so, I change the future. Through these small, intentional choices, I began to see the ripple effects: my daughters laughing more, trusting me again, and our home filling with peace. I can see how far I've come and how much stronger our bond has grown—a living testament to perseverance, humility, and grace.

As you are reading this, I want you to know that while there may be many scars from our past, there is also healing, love, and honesty. You're not alone in grieving the harm your anger may have caused, the ways you've fallen short, or the person you couldn't be when you didn't know how. Grief isn't always about losing others. It's about losing past versions of ourselves and the life we hoped to create in the future. This is okay. It is part of being a human.

Today I call my work *Anger Alchemy*. Like the ancient alchemists who sought to turn base metals into gold, I was learning how to transform anger and grief into wisdom and love. It takes patience, focus, and daily practice—just as those early alchemists failed, experimented, and refined their craft, I learned to do the same with healing my anger.

Working with anger and grief calls you into a deep connection with yourself through the mind, body, and soul. It asks you to listen to your inner voice and what it says about old wounds and core beliefs and to learn new ways of expressing what's been trapped inside. You begin to speak differently, breathe differently, and respond differently. Slowly, the chaos becomes clarity, and the pain becomes power.

The greatest lesson I have learned from this journey, dear reader, is that even when we feel buried beneath the ashes of anger, we can rise. We can emerge wiser, softer, and stronger. Through the alchemy of self-awareness and compassion, our pain becomes our gold, the light that guides us forward, and the legacy we leave for those we love.

TALYA PARDO RICARDO

Talya is a Certified Anger Management Specialist (CAMS-I), Anger Alchemy Coach, and founder of Phoenix Rising. She helps individuals transform anger into a source of power, guiding them to develop emotional intelligence, resilience, and healthier relationships. Talya specializes in understanding the emotional needs of both men and women, helping clients navigate feminine and masculine dynamics with greater clarity and compassion. Her no-nonsense, heart-centered approach empowers others to rise from their emotional challenges and create lasting inner change.

CONNECT WITH TALYA HERE

www.phoenixrisingmentoring.com

www.empoweredgriefjourney.com/tayla

Scan to learn more about Talya

15

SHATTERED BY LOSS, STRENGTHENED BY LOVE

Tanya Bonner

There are defining moments in life that split your world into two. The before and the after. For many years, I felt like I had settled for less than I deserved, wanted, or needed. Then I met Troy, a man who saw me, heard me, and loved me for who I was. He made me laugh with his humour and amazed me with the depths of his knowledge. We shared excitement for the adventures that awaited us and the dream of growing old together.

We started to pave the way forward towards our dreams—hearts on the line—knowing within us that our love was special. I was in the process of packing up the contents of my house, one box at a time, ready to embark on what was next in our love story. Everything was falling into place beautifully and effortlessly. The sparks of electricity, the unity of our hearts, made us both feel whole, a longing both of us wished for, like finding a rare diamond.

One Sunday night, as I reversed my car out of his driveway, I glanced over and caught a glimpse of him tending to his boys. My heart smiled. I already longed to see him again soon. We were both in the throes of preparing our children for their new school year on Monday morning and starting our work week, hoping it would fly by so we could spend the weekend together in our new house that was to be the beginning of blending our families together and making it a home.

The workday was hectic; I barely had a moment to stop and eat lunch. Troy was on my mind, and I couldn't wait to talk to him. Catching my breath, I realized that I hadn't heard from him all day—this was odd and not normal for us. Rushing out of work, I opened my social media. The local news headlines in Warrnambool appeared: there had been an accident with a car and a truck. My heart skipped a beat. I immediately called Troy, but there was no answer. Message after message, I desperately tried to get some sort of response. I hoped that his phone was flat and he had forgotten to take his charger to work, saying to myself, *It's okay, he'll call me soon when he gets home.* Yet... still there was nothing.

Hours passed as I paced the house, desperately checking my phone for a response and frantically calling to find out what was happening. Then there was a knock at the door, a loud, distinctive knock that demanded my attention. I froze for a moment and, reluctantly, opened the door. My eyes locked on the policeman standing there. As I looked at him and heard the words that came from his mouth, I felt my heart and body shatter piece by piece.

I led him through my house, which was filled with cardboard boxes—signs of new beginnings that were also falling apart amid the harsh reality I faced at that moment. I was shaken, physically unwell, crying, and screaming. I couldn't process the words that the police officer said—Troy had been killed in a car accident with a truck while at work today. *What? How? Why?* Our love was perfect—how the hell could something like this be happening to us now? This couldn't be true....

I was rendered completely speechless. I didn't know what to say. In the hours that followed, I couldn't sleep. I just kept pacing and looking up at the stars in the sky, feeling disbelief that this was happening. The world stood still around me, and I cried myself a river. My face was swollen and red from the endless tears streaming down my face. My soul, mind, and body were completely numb. It was a shock that my heart just couldn't comprehend.

I lay in bed, hearing the sound of his voice, wishing that when the sun rose in the morning, everything would be okay. I dozed off briefly before being awoken by police investigators asking me every single horrid question that you could imagine. Trying to find the words to speak, answer, and comprehend what they were saying was simply heart-wrenching.

I developed a fear of driving. It felt like I had also experienced every part of the accident that resulted in his death, and seeing another truck on the road felt horrific and scary. I experienced panic attacks in the car and literally moved my body to dodge every truck that drove by. I hated them. I hated the sound as it went through every part of my body, feeling what Troy must have endured in the final moments of his life.

Two days later, we moved. I couldn't find daycare for my youngest child in our new town, so I drove three hours a day, four days a week, to get him there. It was unimaginably difficult. I had family come with me for support. I would pull over in a mess of tears, my body shaking uncontrollably, and then return home thankful I survived the drive. It felt so wrong that this was happening to me, to us, and to the future we planned together. Our hopes and dreams shattered in a moment, and I was left with every question about why the fuck this was happening. *Why me?* It was perfect…until it wasn't. I reflected on every unimaginable question of the whys in life. I questioned whether I could even go on, since I felt so much pain in my heart. At times, I didn't want to be anywhere except with him. I nearly gave up. It felt wrong to even think of being happy. I didn't want to smile; all I wanted to do was cry and be left alone.

I had a wonderful group of family and friends come to support me and help with the work of moving all the boxes, leaving our life as we knew it behind us. The house that we moved into was large enough for us plus all six of our children, and I was left wondering what living all together would have been like. I avoided the upstairs loungeroom due to the excitement we both had of sitting up there having a drink and a platter of food together once the move was finalised. Being in the house without Troy and his children there shattered me that little bit more.

I was left feeling like a shell, my phone constantly ringing as questions were asked, and the move just happened around me. Days later, I mustered up the courage to tell my children about Troy's death. It was the hardest conversation I've ever had with them. They were shocked and deeply upset, trying to comprehend what had happened, as I comforted them and answered all their questions.

Seeing Troy's children and mine facing their grief was heartbreaking. Even though I was struggling to make sense of his death, I longed to be there for the children, to cry with them, hold them tight in my arms, and tell them that I loved them all a million times over. We stood together side by side, hand in hand, finding love and comfort in being together, an unspoken understanding of the heartache we were all feeling.

In the depths of the darkness, my mind filled with doubt as to whether I could wake up to another day, see someone I love get hurt, or deal with the trivial worries that seemed pointless amongst my current reality. The steps that followed were brutally tough. I was crumbling inside; my body ached with sadness, and everything around me, including the mundane chores of the household, felt like climbing a mountain with every movement taking my breath away and overwhelming my mind. I experienced panic attacks that would leave me lying on the floor in tears or frantically rushing around the house to regain some level of control in my environment, since everything else in my life appeared to be in disarray, chaos, and completely out of my hands.

I pushed myself to visit the accident site, where the grooves from the tyres were deeply etched into the road, and I saw the burnt grass from the fire that had engulfed the truck. The neighbours stood there, picking up pieces of debris and sharing with me the moment they called for help.

I felt an urgency to find out every crucial detail of the accident. I reached out and asked the questions that no one wants the answers to and conversed with the people who were there at the scene of the accident. These were the people who felt the emotions and understood the sheer enormity of the emptiness and loss that I was experiencing.

When I stepped into the funeral home, feelings washed over me as I saw Troy's body lying there. I hyperventilated with pain and cried with heartbreak. Not wanting to leave his side, as I knew the finality of walking out the door, of seeing his face one last time. I kissed his forehead and whispered, "I love you and I always will, no matter what."

I reached out to the truck driver, who also had his life altered that day, trying to offer words of comfort and compassion for his experience. I didn't leave a stone unturned; I experienced it all, and I needed to in order to move forward. I longed for some kind of understanding of what had happened and why.

A few months passed, and I agonised over whether to go on the family holiday that Troy and I had planned together. It dawned on me that I needed to honour our hopes and dreams, even if he wasn't there to walk alongside me; it was exactly what he would want me to do. It was on this holiday that I felt a shift inside of me. After traveling thousands of kilometres to the Gold Coast by car and plane, I arrived at our hotel. When the check-in lady asked me for Troy's driver's licence, I completely broke down, telling her about the accident. She saw the pain in my eyes and simply replied, "It's okay, I'll get it sorted."

As she handed me the key and shared her experience of losing her child, she said, "You will get through this; you'll do this for your children." Our eyes met and connected in the pain that we both knew from our own experiences. This, to me, was like a hand reaching out to my heart, a sign of strength and hope from a stranger who had felt loss yet understood what I needed to continue living.

I had an epiphany when I realised that throughout my life's journey, I had given so much love, kindness, and gratitude to others. I realised it was time to treat myself as I would a best friend and focus on my relationship with myself. This meant focusing on the life I wanted and that Troy believed I deserved.

I chose to live with intention, kindness, love, and connection while also having compassion to nurture my pain and heartache so that I could feel what I needed to without the pressure and constraints of other people's standards. In those silent moments that turned into hours, days, months, and years, my children and I sat in our grief. Some days were overwhelming, so we shifted gears, pivoted, and took steps to choose kindness towards each other and the strangers we would encounter. Knowing the pain and heartache that stripped our souls bare gave us a newfound appreciation for how these acts of kindness and connection to others could truly make a difference.

It inspired us to be a part of the world again. The rays of sunshine, the smiles on faces, the surprise at the random conversations that would develop from a gentle, "Hello, how are you?" These were our glimmers, a symbol of love and hope that we so longed for ourselves and others who had experienced the depths of darkness in their lives.

As I tried to come to grips with my mental well-being, I went back to every moment in my life, observing what I had experienced, the things I had learnt along the way, and how they had brought me to the place where I was now. It felt like I was doing a jigsaw puzzle, trying to appreciate and understand every small piece, and as each piece came together, I realised I was also coming together. I didn't push myself to the limits I had previously because I recognised where I was physically, mentally, and spiritually. I leaned into honouring this space and the time that I truly needed in my grief.

In honouring the loss of my soulmate, Troy, I also learnt that I had to honour myself, and this was my most empowering realisation. He had seen my beauty and whispered the words into my ear, "Don't ever change; you are beautiful just the way you are." Now it was time to start seeing that within myself.

I have learnt the depth of emotions that grief reveals, the impact on myself, and the strength to face my trauma in my mind, body, and spirit, emerging as a stronger and kinder person. The love that Troy and I shared was a moment in time I will forever cherish deep within my soul. After this loss, it felt like parts of me had died with him, yet I was still alive and breathing.

Even when it hurt and didn't make sense, the belief that I had to get comfortable in the uncomfortable and doing whatever it took to comprehend my loss helped pave the way forward. Yes, it was messy, tangled at times like a ball of woolen yarn. Yet, with each pull of the string to untangle the way grief messed up my world, I started to see myself and learn who I really was. One breath, one step at a time, repeated, that led me to where I am today. These steps don't happen all at once. They happen in the sparkles of light, the glimmers when our world seems to be filled with darkness. When we pause to notice those glimmers, we're reminded that we're still here and there's still life waiting to be lived.

Grief is the love we still carry for someone who's no longer here, and sometimes it feels like there's nowhere for that love to go. I gently encourage you to begin by placing that love within you. Hold yourself the way they would have held you. Nurture your heart with the same care you gave them… let it live within you.

TANYA BONNER

Tanya Bonner knows the raw depths of grief—and the strength it takes to rise. After losing her soulmate, she faced the heartbreak of loss while continuing to raise her four children and rebuild her own life. Now a powerful mindset coach, she is passionate about helping other women rise from their own pain into empowerment. Through her story and her work, she turns silence into strength and grief into purpose.

CONNECT WITH TANYA HERE

www.mindsetshift.com.au
www.empoweredgriefjourney.com/tanya

Scan to learn more about Tanya

16

NAVIGATING THE OCEAN OF GRIEF

Serena Mastin

G rowing up, I faced unspeakable abuse, neglect, and shame, leaving my psyche terribly scarred. In the quiet spaces of life, we often come to understand that our emotional wounds shape how we see the world and how we navigate it. We might find ourselves stuck in the same cycles of conflict or struggle, wondering why it always seems to happen. The truth is that we often act based on the patterns we learned in our early years—the emotional wounds that we can't always see clearly but that shape everything. Until we face and heal these wounds, they will keep resurfacing in our lives.

As I transitioned into adulthood, my quest for acceptance and love led me into turbulent relationships, where I inadvertently measured my self-worth by seeking approval from others. I found myself naturally slipping into codependent behaviors, constantly striving to please others and channeling my energy into supporting, nurturing, and shielding them from the consequences of their actions. In doing so, I gradually lost sight of my own identity.

At the age of twenty-nine, after a failed marriage, I found myself as a single mother blessed with two beautiful children. Simultaneously, my career was steadily progressing as I climbed the corporate ladder. My heart became captivated by a profound love for a man who possessed an irresistible charm, keen insight, and an engaging, magnetic personality. Our love was nothing short of electrifying—the kind that stirred the soul, setting our hearts ablaze while providing a profound sense of peace when we were together. Over the next few years, we meticulously mapped out our future, culminating in our marriage and the blending of our families.

Shortly thereafter, I founded an advertising agency, drawing upon more than a decade of marketing experience to forge a new path. My new husband, Kyle, abruptly quit his job and decided to join the agency, overseeing client relationships, travel, and sales. However, the subsequent ten years brought unforeseen challenges, as unresolved issues from our pasts began to cast a shadow over our marriage. Lies, betrayal, and growing resentment marked this gradual downward spiral. Kyle grappled with undiagnosed mental health issues and multiple infidelities, burdening our relationship with pain and turmoil.

Determined to safeguard my marriage, my family, and the business we had built together, I carried the weight of this struggle on my shoulders. The longer I attempted to self-soothe, conceal my pain, and mask my hidden emotions while drawing strength from within, the more I experienced a decline in my physical and mental well-being. This deterioration permeated every facet of my life. I lived under the illusion that I could control and mend everything simply by introspection and identifying my role in fueling the problems. Yet, reality dawned in the quiet moments when I once again found myself concealed, but this time, in a different form, visible yet hidden in plain sight.

I grappled with a profound sense of isolation, unsure of whom to confide in or where to seek solace. Consequently, I endured in silence, downplaying my pain, distancing myself from the love and support of those around me, and harboring my secrets deep within me. The man who once illuminated my world later engulfed it in flames. My love for him had been so all-consuming that it led me to neglect my own well-being and lose sight of my identity in the process.

After navigating through many tumultuous years, I eventually cultivated a heightened self-awareness, recognizing my tendency to conceal my true emotions. It was then that I made a deliberate choice to summon the inner strength required to confront my fears of judgment, shame, criticism, and self-doubt. This newfound clarity gave me the courage to leave my marriage despite the insurmountable risk of losing everything, as I finally prioritized my own well-being and self-preservation.

For too long, I kept my struggles to myself, unwilling to share the weight of my pain. I minimized it, isolated myself, and locked my secrets deep inside, afraid of the judgment and chaos that might follow if the truth came out. One of the hardest things I had to do was tell my team about my divorce. It felt like a betrayal, like I was breaking something important, something I had spent years building. But I knew it was time to face the truth and stand in my vulnerability.

On that cold October afternoon, as I drove to the office, I

couldn't help but notice the fall leaves swirling in the wind, dancing across the ground with each gust of air. My oldest son and his girlfriend, who both worked in the agency, followed me in their car, as I thought about how our team had always felt like family. I wanted to shield them from the devastation of my personal life, but I also knew I couldn't keep pretending anymore. It was time to open up, to be honest, and to step into the power of truth, no matter how humbling or difficult.

With a deep breath, I walked through the double doors of the office, my heart racing. The tension in the room was palpable. I could feel their eyes on me, waiting for me to speak. The silence felt deafening, like every droplet of water from the bathroom faucet echoed throughout the space, creating a rhythm that mirrored the chaos in my mind. But I swallowed my fears and spoke up, sharing my truth.

"I promised to always be fully transparent with you," I began, my voice shaking but firm. "Yet, in my effort to protect each of you, I have withheld the truth. Kyle and I are getting a divorce. It has been a difficult journey, but I had to make hard decisions for my well-being, my children, and the future of this company."

Everyone in the room stood still, processing my words. I could feel the weight of their emotions. Some sighed, others shook their heads in disbelief, but all of them were alert and present. I continued, "I am feeling empowered now. For the first time in years, I can finally breathe. The kids are resilient, and I know God has a bigger plan for us. The agency will thrive because of you. I believe in every single one of you."

As I spoke, the room filled with energy, questions, concerns, and reassurance all blended together. But despite the uncertainty and challenges, I stood my ground, offering strength to my team. I knew that we had a choice: to let this moment break us, or to rise above it.

After the meeting, I went to the kitchen and grabbed a bottle of champagne, hoping to release some of the tension that had built up inside me. I raised my glass with a smile and said, "Cheers to new beginnings!" We clinked glasses, and for a moment, it felt like everything would be okay.

But as the excitement settled, I overheard my team whispering about Kyle and an employee who had recently left the agency. The words stung more than I expected, and I stepped in quickly, reminding them that gossip had no place here. My oldest son spoke up, his voice weak but certain. "Mom, they're not gossiping," he said, his pale face and clouded eyes betraying the pain he was feeling. "It's true. Kyle was with her, too."

The blow to my chest felt like a bomb exploding, shattering everything I thought I knew. How could Kyle—the only father he had ever known—let our son carry that burden? How could he be so reckless in front of my son? As the room began to spin, I tried to gather myself, but the weight of those words suffocated me.

My employees, all of them, had known. They had seen the signs, the tension, the lies. And I was left standing there, exposed and broken. "We thought you knew," they said, their words like daggers. The lies that had been hidden from me for so long were now spilling out, unraveling everything I thought was secure. But in that moment, I realized something important. Despite the hurt, despite the betrayal, I was stronger than I had ever been.

In the weeks following Kyle's departure from my life, the storm didn't let up. The weight of lies unraveling around me, coupled with the chaos of living in a hotel with my children, was a relentless burden. I had to navigate selling the house, informing clients of the changes, and somehow creating a sense of normalcy for my kids. But with every step forward, the challenges grew heavier.

Kyle's actions escalated; he tried to tear down the business and destroy the relationships we had worked so hard to build. It felt like my entire world was being torn apart, and yet, I refused to let his actions dictate my future. Even in the face of financial devastation and endless gossip, I kept moving forward. My resolve was unwavering, and the support that poured in from peers, clients, and family helped me stay grounded. But as the truth about Kyle's reckless behavior surfaced, it became even harder to process. The lies, the deceit, the destruction—it was a whirlwind of pain. But one thing became clear: the truth had set me free.

Late one evening, as I lay in bed, tossing and turning, I felt the exhaustion in my body, but my mind refused to quiet. The flicker of the streetlight outside my window only added to the restless feeling that gripped me. I stumbled down the hall, hoping a warm bath would soothe me. Just before dipping my toe into the bathwater, a notification buzzed on my phone. I hesitated, wondering who could be messaging me so late. Wrapped in a towel, I reached for my phone to read the message. It was from Kyle.

I'm so sorry for all the pain I caused you, and I am grateful for all the memories we shared.

It was three in the morning. I couldn't help but wonder why he was awake at this hour. But then, as I read those words, a wave of warmth washed over me. Could this be the apology I had longed for? The beginning of some healing between us? The possibility of reconciliation flickered in my heart, and I quickly began typing my response.

But then I paused.

As I sat there, heart racing, I realized the gravity of my decision. I couldn't blindly open my heart to someone who had caused me so much pain. So, instead I composed a simple reply:

Thank you, Kyle. That means the world to me. I appreciate you thinking of me.

After a few minutes of staring at the glowing screen, waiting for a response that never came, I sank into the warmth of the bath. The weight of the day still lingered, but I eventually found solace under the covers, falling into an exhausted sleep.

The next morning, sunlight peeked through the blinds, and I rubbed my eyes, stretching as I reached for my phone. I expected Kyle's response. Instead, I saw several missed calls from an unknown number. The voice on the voicemail was frantic, hysterical. My heart raced as I tried to decipher the words. Something wasn't right, and then, through the garbled message, I heard, "You need to go to the hospital. Now."

I didn't waste a second. Panic surged as I scrambled out of bed, pulling myself together and grabbing my keys. I drove as fast as I could, my mind spinning, trying to make sense of the cryptic message.

As I entered the hospital, the cold silence of the empty halls sent a chill through me. The antiseptic smell hung heavily in the air, mixing with the scent of cleaning products. I rushed to the front desk, slid my ID across the counter, and asked for Kyle's room number. As the attendant dialed, I waited, pacing back and forth in the empty waiting room. The beeping of medical devices and muffled voices from the hallway echoed around me, creating an atmosphere of tension.

Finally, a knock at the door broke the silence. A physician's assistant entered, accompanied by an officer in a muted black suit. The room seemed to close in around me as I struggled to stay composed. The doctor's face was somber as she spoke those words that would forever alter my reality: Kyle had taken his own life.

The ground beneath me felt like it had disappeared, and a sharp pain gripped my chest. I could barely breathe as I stared up at the fluorescent light flickering above me. It was as though I had become detached from my body, unable to process what was happening. A long moment of silence followed.

The years I spent trying to protect Kyle, trying to save him from himself, all seemed to lead to this moment. I couldn't save him. I had loved him so much that I lost myself in the process, giving up pieces of my identity in the hope of making him whole again. I would have given anything to save him, to bring him back to the man I once knew. But it was too late.

In the days that followed, I was left grappling with the weight of his actions, the lies, the destruction, the painful truth that he had left behind. And yet, I realized that the most profound part of this journey was the strength I found within myself. I had spent so long protecting him, hiding my pain, and trying to hold everything together. But in the wake of his death, I was forced to confront the truth, and in doing so, I began to rebuild.

I found healing in accepting the ugliness of the truth. It wasn't easy, and it didn't come without pain, but it was the key to my freedom. In the end, I realized that while I couldn't save Kyle, I could save myself. In doing so, I could create a future not defined by the past but by the strength and resilience that emerged from the darkest of moments.

Today, I stand as a survivor, having confronted the harrowing shadows of isolation, devastation, and victimization that once entangled me. My children are healthy and thriving; I find joy in watching them pursue their dreams. Throughout this transformative journey, I found my true calling, to inspire those suffering, enduring, numbing their pain, masking their scars, or guarding their hearts, empowering them to discover their voices and reveal their authentic stories.

Until you heal the wounds of your past, they will bleed into every aspect of your life. You might attempt to conceal, isolate, numb, or repress these emotions, but ultimately, you must summon the courage to uncover your wounds, revealing the root of the pain that impedes your progress. Confront the memories, reconcile with them, and, in doing so, find the ability to release them and gently move forward. The truth about trauma is that it leaves a tangible imprint on your body. So, when you close your eyes and recall a painful memory, your body serves as a constant reminder that it's still there.

I recognized the need for healing, but discussing it was merely the initial step; for me, the most agonizing part was writing the explicit details and revealing aspects of my life I had concealed for so long. As arduous as this process proved to be, it was also immensely healing. Page by page, chapter by chapter, in my memoir called *Exposed: You Can't Heal When You Hide*, I released the raw, vulnerable details of my life. I shattered old patterns, shed my shame, and finally took ownership of my narrative. It was my story and mine alone to recount. I had the option to keep it hidden or bravely expose my scars by sharing the most intimate experiences of my life, in hopes that someone, even just one person, would hear my story, feel less alone, let go of their shame, and find the courage deep within themselves to reclaim their power and own their own story.

When we keep our stories locked away, they begin to decay

within us, affecting our actions, choices, health, and well-being. Revealing my true history stung, and every instinct urged me to conceal it again, but something unexpected happened: healing emerged. Sharing my story and bringing it into the light, vulnerably laying bare my soul, allowed those infected wounds to begin healing themselves. Recounting these memories was heart-wrenching but also a source of heart-healing. I no longer viewed myself as burdened by shame; instead, I saw a different version of myself. I saw a young girl, a rebellious teenager, an inexperienced young woman, and a self-sacrificing mother. I saw someone who had been damaged but was still deserving of love, happiness, and healing. I saw someone with the courage to survive, determined never to give up. I saw someone who had fought for her children, her family, and those she cherished most and, in some way, without even realizing it, had fought for herself.

I didn't paint myself as a victim of circumstances or demonize others. Instead, I embraced my journey, and in doing so, I developed a profound love for myself. I welcomed my mistakes, extended forgiveness, altered behavioral patterns, and authentically uncovered a new purpose. However, I didn't navigate these waters alone; I surrounded myself with those who inspired, challenged, and empowered me to continue growing despite obstacles. I firmly believe that each of us possesses a unique story to tell—waiting for us to grasp and embrace imperfections, broken promises, and mistakes, and all, with open, loving arms, offering ourselves the healing we deserve. Upon reflection, I am deeply grateful for the incredible individuals who enveloped me in unconditional love and unwavering support when I couldn't see beyond my tears. They lifted me up when I couldn't stand on my own, investing their time and energy in supporting my vision as I navigated my healing journey.

One statement resonated profoundly deep within my heart: *You don't have to sacrifice yourself to earn the affection or approval of others.* So often, I had sacrificed my own needs for the sake of others, laboring under the self-limiting belief that my worth hinged on what I could give rather than who I am. This simple yet profound statement has allowed me to understand that my value doesn't diminish based on someone else's inability to recognize my worth.

In my closing thoughts, I reflect on how the stars rise after the darkness descends, the sun rises after the night falls, a flower emerges from the earth after its seeds are buried, and with every stumble in life, we grow with more extraordinary grace, patience, compassion, and wisdom than ever before. As an advocate for healing and an empathic leader, I have a wealth of post-traumatic wisdom to share, having navigated through the peaks and valleys of life and entrepreneurship, drawing inspiration from the most tenacious and influential women in the world. These formidable women have lived in the trenches, endured profound pain, made their share of mistakes, weathered numerous failures, and though they've been shattered, they remain relentless and fearless. Rather than succumbing to adversity, it ignites their spirit. They rise above, extend forgiveness, love deeply, and pour their hearts into everything they undertake.

This transformation characterizes the woman I've become and has guided me toward my purpose: to empower others to take ownership of their stories, look inward, embrace healing, stop hiding, and boldly step into their power.

One way to approach this journey is with my acronym OCEAN, which has served as my guiding light and helped me process my grief:

OCEAN
Navigating Grief

O – Overcoming the Waves: Grief comes in waves, sometimes gentle, sometimes overwhelming. It's important to allow yourself to feel what you're feeling, acknowledging your emotions and letting them pass through you.

C – Connecting with Others: You don't have to grieve alone. Seek out friends, family, or a support group. Connection is crucial, especially when the pain feels unbearable.

E – Embracing the Pain: Healing begins when we stop resisting the pain. It's okay to feel sadness, anger, and confusion. These emotions are part of the journey, and embracing them is the first step toward healing.

A – Accepting Change: Life after loss is different. But in that difference, there is room for growth. Finding new meaning and purpose is part of the process of moving forward.

N – Navigating a New Normal: Grief changes you. But it doesn't define you. With each small step forward, you begin to create a life where the love you've lost and the healing you seek can coexist.

Grief isn't a burden you need to carry alone. It's a season that, when moved through with intention and support, can reveal your inner resilience. By addressing your emotional needs, recognizing patterns, and following a structured path toward healing, you can honor the memory of your loved one while also reclaiming your life. Obstacles and sorrow are inherent in the journey of life; we all encounter difficulties, and sometimes, life reveals an unfamiliar aspect of ourselves. Remember—what is causing you pain is also fostering your growth. What burdens you is imparting valuable lessons. When you eventually take a moment to contemplate your path, you might not even identify the individual you've transformed into. Instead, you'll start recognizing the person you were destined to be, armed with greater clarity, courage, strength, and resilience. This transformation could be the most precious gift you ever receive. No matter how your story began, you hold the power to change the path and write a new ending.

SERENA MASTIN

Serena's career has included being knocked down and climbing back to executive leadership roles with Fortune 500 companies. In 2013, she founded Pulse Marketing Inc., an award-winning marketing and advertising agency. In addition to being a visionary entrepreneur, Serena recently published her first book, *Exposed: You Can't Heal When You Hide*, a memoir recounting her life story in harrowing detail. She has dedicated her life to personally and professionally empowering others.

CONNECT WITH SERENA HERE

www.serenamastin.com
www.empoweredgriefjourney.com/serena

Scan to learn more about Serena

17

TORN BY GRIEF, TETHERED BY LOVE

Linda Henderson

The moment I realized my daughter Andrea was gone, my life split in two—before and after. The world around me continued to move, but my world remained frozen. There are no words that fully capture the sound of a mother's heartbreak or the quiet that follows when her child's presence becomes a memory. Child loss is unnatural and unfair. My grief didn't just visit, it moved into every fiber of my existence. It crushed me, rearranged who I was, and left me defeated. My story is one of devastating loss, but also about what grief taught me and the painful and transformative journey that ultimately led me to hope.

Andrea was the younger of my two daughters. As a child, she had long, soft, curly blond hair that darkened slightly as she grew, but her beauty never faded; if anything, it deepened. Her sky-blue eyes held a sparkle that stopped people in their tracks, drawing compliments from strangers who felt the softness of her spirit and her captivating beauty. She had this quiet little giggle, a laugh that barely made a sound yet lit up every room. Andrea's presence was like a tender flame—never loud, never demanding, but always warm. She wasn't just my daughter. She was my mirror, my morning light, my confidante. It was a blessing to witness her transform into a remarkable woman and be part of that journey. I learned from her in so many ways.

I recall adult conversations where her words gave me the confidence to rely on my faith and strength. One of my most precious memories is of going out to a restaurant for lunch with her and her baby boy. As we both fed him bites of food from our plates, I said, "Now you know how much I love you," and her reply was, "I know, Mamma." We supported and comforted one another, and she stood by my side when life grew heavy. She was love in its purest, simplest form.

Married, the mother of a two-year-old boy, and pregnant with her second child, Andrea was a social worker. She was very excited to be in her new house with her growing family. She worked for a group home serving the youth of our community and taught in their literacy program. On December 20, 2011, she was in Belleville, Ontario, with her coworker. They were guiding a couple of young girls who had raised funds to "adopt" a child to provide Christmas gifts for. Part of her role was to help shape these girls into admirable citizens.

Andrea and her coworker were filled with joy and eager to return to work and reflect on the day's meaningful impact. They were in their car, a few blocks away from returning to the group home, and were waiting to turn left onto the next street. Andrea was a front-seat passenger, and her coworker was the driver. A transport truck driver, who was texting while driving, hit the car from behind. This impact pushed their car into the oncoming traffic, where they collided with another vehicle. Both the driver and my daughter died instantly.

One moment, she was here—my anchor, my joy, my constant—and the next, she was gone. The anguish of losing Andrea is deeply embedded forever in my soul. There are no words that can describe the gut-wrenching, agonizing screams that this trauma caused me. It was as if the air disappeared from my lungs. I didn't know how, nor did I want to breathe in a world that no longer held her. Time became meaningless. The sun still rose, and people still moved, but I felt trapped in a nightmare I couldn't wake up from. I remember comparing my existence to that of a robot. I ate and moved according to my husband's direction in those early days. Like the devastation of an earthquake, all I could feel was my world crushed into thousands of pieces beneath my feet. The warmth she gave so freely had vanished, and I was left to survive in the cold darkness of grief. I did not know how I would move from one breath to the next, let alone survive.

Without warning, my world, as I once knew it, was changed forever. Grief ravaged my life and destroyed my sense of security, confidence, and stability. Grief is ugly, raw, and relentless. Grief does not ask for permission and knows no boundaries. It stole my daughter like a thief in the night. I struggled to move from one moment to the next when submerged in the deep, suffocating waters of sorrow. Confusion, hopelessness, numbness, and emptiness are some words that describe the state I was in. I was detached and unable to connect with the world surrounding me.

Grief is not just one feeling; it's a complex combination of emotions, including sadness, anger, guilt, fear, depression, anxiety, and countless others. These emotions can come in waves that suddenly overwhelm and drown a person. At the time, I did not know that these feelings were acceptable and that I was not going crazy. I remember feeling like my brain could not function anymore. The rage, fogginess, forgetfulness, and not being able to stop the tears long enough to think are frightening.

Grief is as unique as a fingerprint. There is no timeline. You are not alone, and there is no right or wrong way to handle this process. These are things I needed to learn. Emotionally, I felt heartbroken and hopeless, and I cried endless tears. When I reflect on those early days now, I didn't think a person could produce so many tears. I recall the hoarseness I developed from all the screaming. Depression and anxiety attacked and controlled every movement of my body. Whether I was in a parking lot, a grocery store, or anywhere, the triggers would interrupt the moment and transport me to the darkest part of my world. Physically, I was exhausted. Frustration added to my daily struggle of not keeping up with what was expected of me on a typical day. Grief is strenuous work; the body responds with insomnia, or too much sleep, and overeating, or not eating enough. The standard activities of daily living were beyond my grasp.

Mentally, I couldn't concentrate or find words to express my needs. My ability to process information or to have a conversation was almost non-existent. I felt my heart beating and the movement of life around me, but I was on the outside looking in at my existence. Spiritually, I lost all my faith; I was angry at God for taking my daughter. My belief system about life and death became shattered. There was a moment in the early days of my grief when the weight of loss became unbearable. I disappeared—physically and emotionally—seeking solitude, silence, and perhaps, a final escape.

I walked to a quiet, open field, where the world around me was blurred by my misery. I sat alone, surrounded by nothing but my sorrow, and contemplated ending it all. I didn't want to leave my family, and I did not want to die, but I felt helpless and could not be consumed with pain for one more minute. I prayed; I argued with my God until my physical strength deserted me. Then something stopped me. Not a grand voice or a sudden revelation—just a flicker of something I can only describe as hope. A quiet realization that if I let go, I would be leaving behind not just my pain, but the memory, the love, the truth of my daughter Andrea.

So, I stood up, bereaved but breathing. I walked back home with no clear answers, but with one decision: I would survive. Not all at once, but piece by piece. I chose to face grief—not conquer it, but live with it, learn from it, and eventually carry it with strength. That day didn't take me. Instead, it became the beginning of a transformation I could never have imagined. I describe this day as the most profound, pivotal moment in my journey toward recovery.

I desperately needed hope, the anchor in the journey of grief. Hope is not about expecting the pain to vanish, but about believing you can find purpose again one day. It is not a denial of the loss, but rather a quiet belief that a better future is possible, despite the profound pain. Hope is the key to resilience and rebuilding a life that has changed. Hope must be cultivated, like embers glowing that can ignite brightness in the dark, even amid unimaginable despair. In my journey, I searched for a way forward, while honoring my daughter and our love. I discovered that three essential pillars—acknowledgment, action, and appreciation—gave me a foundation for healing and helped me reclaim hope.

In my grief, acknowledgment became the moment I faced a truth too heavy for words—my daughter Andrea was never coming home. I would never see her smile, hear her voice, or feel her warm embrace again. I screamed from a place I didn't know existed until my body collapsed over and over again. The pain was a storm that ripped through my soul and every cell of my being. The stillness that followed wasn't peace, but paralysis. I remember feeling numb and unsure how to move from one space to another. I learned that I had to unravel all the emotions. To scream, to feel the anger that burned and the fear that trembled beneath it. I had to honor every raw emotion without apology. I learned that naming the pain didn't make it grow stronger—it made room for me to understand and let healing begin. Acknowledgment became my first act of love, both for her and for myself.

When we begin the unthinkable process of feeling the emotions, it validates the pain, love, and relationship. It is vital not to rush through or hide the pain; be patient and gentle when giving grief space. Grief is a deeply personal experience and does not follow a predictable pattern. Understand that it takes time and repetition, and expect both good and bad days. Acknowledgment is the challenging but crucial first step in the process of moving forward and opening the space for light.

Hope doesn't just happen; it starts with a slight glimmer in the darkness. Cultivating hope is like planting seeds that must be nurtured and cared for, and then with time we see the growth. We need to nurture hope with actions, patience, and perseverance. Remember that action doesn't have to be a grand motion. It starts with setting small, achievable goals that create momentum toward hope and decrease the weight of grief.

Whatever these small actions look like, simply doing them has power. They can be as simple as making your bed, brushing your teeth, or drinking fluids. What started for me as a simple step to look out my door and feel the warmth of the sun led to regular walking, which became my tool for healing. Through this coping skill, my book *The Road of Love & Hope: The Journey of Child Loss* came to fruition.

Whatever the actions look like for you, they move you out of the dark moment toward hope. Remember to celebrate progress as small victories. Give yourself compassion with respect, and accept setbacks.

In the aftermath of losing Andrea, I found that appreciation became one of the most powerful pillars that held my hope. As I navigated my loss, acknowledged my feelings, and created small, positive actions, I experienced clarity and strength. As I moved through my pain to make space for life again, I realized that love and grief can co-exist. I appreciate and treasure the moments I had with my daughter. What we shared is a blessing and reminds me of our forever bond and love. It echoes on my road of grief, whispering in the quiet and steadying me in the storm. Appreciation is quiet and felt in the small moments. Walking and being immersed in nature bring me peace and solace. Chirping birds, the scents of nature, and the warmth of the sun create a grounding in the present. The most significant lesson that grief has taught me is that life is a gift. Yesterday is gone, and tomorrow may never come; today is the only piece of time that we can control. I take my broken pieces, secured together with love, and strive to see the beauty around me. I rise with resilience and courage, driven by a new purpose to inspire and empower.

When we nurture gratitude, we nurture hope.
Embrace the moments.
Cherish the memories.
Hope for tomorrow.

LINDA HENDERSON

Linda Henderson is a retired nurse with thirty-seven years of experience in compassionate care. After the tragic loss of her adult daughter Andrea, she found her new purpose in helping others navigate the complex journey of grief. She holds certifications in Professional Grief and Bereavement, Coping with Child Loss, and Grief and Bereavement Counseling. Linda is the author of a memoir called *The Road of Love & Hope* and the creator of the Triple-A framework—Acknowledgment, Action, and Appreciation—offering guidance to those seeking hope after loss.

CONNECT WITH LINDA HERE

www.authorlindahenderson.com
www.empoweredgriefjourney.com/linda

Scan to learn more about Linda

18

THE JOURNEY BACK TO ME
HEALING AND RECLAIMING JOY AFTER ABUSE

Dawn Michele Jackson

*I remember what it was like to find my way out of the
dark after not knowing how I found myself in that
place—a place I was afraid to talk about and
didn't yet have the tools to navigate.*

As I look at my life in the rearview mirror, I've come to realize that for many years, I was not aware of the profound impact abuse had on my life, nor of the darkness that had cast its shadow over me.

I don't truly remember the beginning of the abuse that somehow found itself shoved into the corners of my mind, locked away with no key. But I do know that emotional, verbal, and physical abuse became a "normal" part of my existence as a teenager in an unhealthy romantic relationship.

I was a quiet, reserved student in high school, dedicated to my studies and staying out of trouble. I experienced enough hardship in my home life, navigating alcoholism with my father and my stepfather. I'd come to realize that the best thing to do was to expect the unexpected. My nervous system continually functioned in fight-or-flight mode, ready for the next impending crisis to appear.

Addiction never waits for a good day to rear its ugly head. When I'd find myself finally taking a deep breath and hoping there might be a moment of calm, the addict would come home drunk, belligerent, and ready to stir up tension in the household. My mom constantly tried to shield me from the impact it had on my childhood. But unfortunately, I grew up believing that this level of drama was normal and every family experienced it.

Being the well-behaved, responsible child who was trying not to make any waves felt lonely at times. I often kept to myself and found comfort in only a handful of close friends. I kept most people at a distance, afraid to bring my friends home, fearing my stepdad might show up under the influence again. Addiction never brings out the best in those we love, and this situation was no different. I craved the times when he was sober and showing up with his kind heart, loving me unconditionally.

As a high school sophomore, feeling a sense of sadness in my soul and yearning for connection, I was flattered when a senior took notice of me. It didn't take long before I jumped into what would become the most devastating relationship of my life.

I couldn't fathom that someone older would want to date me or even invite me to his prom. The attention felt wonderful at first—I was on top of the world.

Unfortunately, as our relationship developed, his controlling behavior became more apparent. If he couldn't manipulate me to get his needs met, verbal and physical abuse followed. Fear became my constant companion.

The relationship with my boyfriend began to feel suffocating. The fear I encountered every day left me feeling trapped and powerless. I desperately tried to make him happy so I wouldn't encounter his dark side once again. Over time, his manipulative behavior convinced me I couldn't navigate life without his presence. My self-esteem plummeted.

During my first few years of college, I made the long drive home nearly every weekend to see my boyfriend, fearing if I didn't, he'd leave me or worse. Our phone calls involved continual cycles of him ending our relationship, only to beg for reconciliation days later. It was a vicious cycle, yet every time I tried to break free, he threatened to take his own life. And there were the times he actually cut his wrists, which left me feeling desperate to somehow make things right.

Looking back, I felt ashamed for not leaving or crying out for help. I remember locking myself in the bathroom to escape his wrath, only to have him punch a hole in the door. I felt sheer terror as I prayed for my life. One time, I jumped out of his truck while it was moving and I ran into the woods to escape. I was always too afraid to keep running and would return to his presence, thinking somehow things would change.

Things never changed for the better; they only escalated for the worse, and despite this fact, he eventually proposed to me while I was attending college. My angels were working overtime and delivered a loud, clear message to me—I could not marry this man. At that point, I refused to accept his proposal (despite my fears) and slowly began to pull away, knowing that someday I'd end up dead if I didn't find a way out.

Emotionally, I had detached from my abusive boyfriend by the time I was introduced to my future husband. But physically detaching was another story. The last straw was him banging on our sliding glass door, trying desperately to get to me. Thankfully, my stepfather arrived home in time to intervene; however, I lived in fear for years wondering if my ex would ever come after me. My physical safety became my top priority and still is to this day.

Finding freedom and gratitude in releasing this abusive individual from my life, I soon found myself in a relationship with a kind, gentle, loving man that would eventually lead to marriage. Sadly, I had no tools to help me navigate my prior abusive relationship, nor did I realize that I was moving my boxes of hurt, sadness, and anger into our home.

My husband found it difficult to understand my anger because, frankly, I didn't understand it either. It felt like every thought, feeling, and experience from my past was buried in a locked room with shadows lurking underneath the door, seeping out into my life.

My pain transferred into my need to control and make sure everything was perfect. There was no room for missteps in my life; however, I perpetually created my own drama because it's what I'd lived for years, and it felt normal. Life wasn't lived without drama, or so I believed at that time.

After our son was born, my marriage deteriorated, and my husband asked for a divorce. I immediately dove into anger, blaming him for abandoning me and choosing to give up. My world spiraled into darkness again, yet I still couldn't "see" the path that led me to this point.

Feeling heartbroken, devastated, alone, depressed, and stuck, somehow I managed to get through each day while crying behind closed doors at night after my son went to bed. I prayed my husband would change his mind and reconcile with me, but that never happened.

Not knowing how to pull myself out of the hole I found myself in, I started focusing outward and putting my energy toward helping less-fortunate individuals. As a nurse, joining surgical mission trips to underdeveloped countries filled my heart and brought me joy for a while. But over time, I noticed that I continued to struggle with emotional pain. As I look back, I realize that I lacked awareness and the tools that would lead to healing my heart at that point in my life.

As I limped along, dear friends of mine began encouraging my spiritual growth while gently taking my hand and walking beside me. Each new class, workshop, or training provided new tools, reflection, and healing, but I still found myself wondering why joy was fleeting and rarely resided in my heart. My husband left me with a beautiful home, I was raising an incredible son, my job gave me the ability to live a comfortable life, and I had a family that loved me. But something inside didn't feel right. Was there something wrong with me?

Eventually, I found myself enrolled in a training program to become certified as a Grief Recovery Method Specialist. It sounded like something that might benefit me, although I didn't completely believe that grief was an issue in my life. That all changed on the first day of training!

Within the first hour, I remember coming to the sad realization that my life had been filled with grieving experiences, starting in early childhood. However, I still had no idea how much that grief had cast its shadow over everything in my life, including my relationships and how I felt about myself.

I'd locked up so much pain in my heart for years; it was my coping mechanism, keeping me safe and alive. Sadly, suppressing the pain only perpetuated it and led to unhealthy ways to navigate my life.

While there were many layers of grief to heal in my life, the one that led to my greatest freedom was healing from the abuse I suffered as a teenager. Somehow, I'd come to feel ashamed of myself for not walking away from that relationship. Thoughts surfaced like:

You should have known better.
How could you let this happen?
Maybe you deserved it.
His parents witnessed it and didn't report it, so maybe it wasn't that bad.
You never ended up in the hospital.
I'm sure others have it much worse.

I questioned myself about why I hadn't spoken up about the abuse or reached out for help. Shame hit the top of the list, followed by a fear that my loved ones wouldn't believe me or would minimize my experience. I was drowning inside and determined not to let anyone push me further down.

Continual feelings of anger, shame, and sadness filled my life. But looking back, I realize the universe was always gently guiding me to the support and healing I needed and deserved. For the first time in many, many years, I gained tools from the Grief Recovery Method to navigate, heal, and transform my life.

I remember what it was like to find my way out of the dark after not knowing how I found myself in that place—a place I was afraid to talk about and didn't yet have the tools to navigate. For years, I didn't realize that I was only a few steps away from seeing the light and stepping out of the darkness.

I stepped out of the prison I'd found myself in and away from that terrified young girl I'd been for years. I stepped into the empowered woman I am today and into a new world full of opportunities, love, and support.

I was able to let go of the anger that had been keeping me hostage. I experienced inner peace again. And I found the joy that had been constantly eluding me for so long.

I realized that without healing my heart, the pain affected every aspect of my life and relationships. It was impossible to create peace around me when I wasn't experiencing it inside myself.

I realized that healing wasn't about forgetting or condoning; it was about reclaiming my power. And by taking back my power, I took back my life.

This wasn't easy! For years, my life had been surrounded by drama externally and internally. In the beginning, I felt uneasy experiencing calm, peaceful moments. Constantly reminding myself that I was safe versus waiting for the next shoe to drop was sometimes an hourly exercise.

Fast-forward to today, I've learned that despite events and circumstances around me, I can maintain my inner peace and calm. Drama no longer feels comfortable or inviting but instead feels very uncomfortable and is something I choose to minimize in my life.

I've come to realize that every aspect of my journey has been an incredible gift in my life. Without these experiences, I wouldn't be who I am today or have the same compassion and dedication to helping others heal.

The abuse taught me about my strength and my worth. It showed me what I deserve and the importance of setting boundaries. It gave me eyes of empathy and a loving heart to support others.

My husband's leaving gave me the wings to grow, heal, and fly. On some level, his soul knew that my wings were clipped and that part of his journey was to help release them and allow me to fly again. I know without a doubt that had he stayed, I would have continued focusing on my roles as a nurse, mom, and wife, and neglected my broken heart.

Finding myself again was one of the greatest gifts of my life. As I look back over the last fifty-plus years of my life, I smile at who I've become. I'm proud of the woman who stands tall, believes in herself, and allows her voice to be heard.

I realize that I'm not what happened to me, nor are you.

I'm grateful for the pain, the healing, and the gifts that have shaped my life today. Our life experiences and trauma are a page in our book, but never the whole story. You hold the power to change your life and your story through healing your heart.

As you move forward on your journey, I invite you to focus on the light as you step out of the darkness that's been holding you back, my friend. I believe in you and hope you soon discover how much joy is waiting right around the corner for you!

DAWN MICHELE JACKSON

Dawn Jackson, RN, is an Advanced Grief Recovery Method Specialist and bestselling author who draws on more than 30 years of nursing experience to help individuals heal, transform, and rediscover joy. Through her compassionate work, Dawn guides others from surviving to thriving, empowering them to embrace wellness in mind, body, and spirit. She is the author of *Journey to Peace and Healing and Journey to Self Discovery: 100 Days of Soulful Reflections*. Her work has been featured in *Aspire Magazine*, on TUT.com, in several international bestselling anthologies, and on numerous podcasts.

CONNECT WITH DAWN HERE

www.dawnmichelejackson.com
www.empoweredgriefjourney.com/dawn

Scan to learn more about Dawn

19

MY FUTURE DIED, BUT MY LIFE IS NOT OVER

Lisa Woolery

One day, my husband Eric died. He just dropped dead, while I was chopping broccoli, actually. As I made dinner, he was in his office down the hall returning work calls and emails. A few minutes earlier, I'd met him at the door with a big kiss. He told me there were so many good things in his day. He would tell me them all later.

I never did find out what they were.

I was fixing another mundane meal because we were dieting, so I decided to go and tell him a joke, "Dinner will be so boring—broccoli again—you might fall asleep." He would laugh because he is still delighted in me after twenty-eight years. We would discuss our Mrs. Dash seasoning options.

The hallway felt deathly quiet.

Turns out, it was.

I opened the door and found my husband—my everything, the love of my life, my best friend, my protector, my cheerleader, my dinner partner, my high school sweetheart, the father of my children, my future, my past, my retirement, the one I would celebrate my fiftieth wedding anniversary with—dead.

I picked up his phone and screamed into it to the 911 dispatcher.

Paramedics took three or four minutes to arrive.

How long is three or four minutes? Forever when I am giving my husband CPR.

Is My Life Over?

The next day as I walked down the hall, no doubt to do a task for one of my tweens, a thought stopped me in my tracks.

Literally stopped me.

Lisa, your life is over.

WHAT? I replied to myself. *I guess it is.*

I mean, it was a good life… but what could possibly come next?

That landed like a bowling ball in my stomach, adding to the heaviness I already felt.

A Comeback?

A few months later, the lady from our grief group called to tell me that one of my children wasn't invited back for Wednesday night pizza and age-appropriate grief exercises. It was like they had never dealt with an angry tween before. A boy who had just lost his everything…

Honestly, I was okay with it. I told her none of us would be returning. The call made me consider that Wednesday evenings for me had been just sitting in a room listening to sad people talk about how they were stuck. My kids told me they felt their answers had to be "happy."

This wasn't how we were meant to grieve.

After that, instead, on Wednesdays, my little family visited a nearby park. The kids played their bodies to exhaustion, while I obsessively finished my 20,000 steps to do the same for myself.

We did our own healing regime, we prayed together, and we allowed all thoughts and conversations. As long as we were not being unkind to one another, we could say anything, and we did. I sent my kids out to the backyard sometimes to scream and rage, to throw things, to break things, to feel the hard ground on their bodies. We needed to grieve hard because what we lost meant something—everything, it seemed.

As I obsessively walked, my steps beat out these words: *I will not let Eric's death kill me too. I will orchestrate my comeback.*

With no idea of how, I decided I would do stuff without censoring myself. This meant I cried in Target if I needed to. I said no when normal things felt too big. I said yes to everyone who called and asked to take me to lunch or coffee. I accepted help and felt like a part of the community who wanted to help us.

The Vision Board

My first New Year's Eve as a widow was not totally dismal because I was at my best friend's house. As kids ran around and adults watched music videos and drank fun drinks, I sat in the middle of it all, focused. Totally focused. My BFF sat me at the kitchen table with a pile of magazines so high I couldn't even see over it. I obsessively paged through, tearing and cutting out pictures.

Who do I want to be?

I hung my vision board in my throne (toilet) room. Each time I tinkled, I looked up at yoga poses, roasted vegetables, clinking wine glasses, hiking boots, typewriters, and suitcases. The beautiful thing about a vision board is that there are no deadlines for your "goals," and by pasting them on a board you have given yourself permission to say yes when an opportunity gets presented to you.

One of my first opportunities was a hiking club. First, know that it took me months to actually attend the group I joined. That's okay. I needed to mentally catch up with my idea.

I love hiking, but I had no one to hike with. One warm spring day, I finally showed up. I got out of my car, stood in the circle, sprayed my skin for bugs, joined the circle of hikers, and introduced myself. Twenty minutes into the hike, I blurted, "My husband died!"

I felt so conspicuous because the man who had been at my side for over half of my life was gone.

Did anyone notice? Of course not, but to me it was like I lost my whole right side, hiking without a right arm, hopping along on my left leg.

I was mortified. No one really cared though—they all just hiked along, and one man walked next to me and let me tell my story. Six years later, I still see that guy from time to time. He still says hello and doesn't outwardly treat me like a freak.

I slowly said yes to things on my vision board, and those brave steps led to other brave steps.

Give Yourself Grace and Time

One of the things that always shows up on my vision boards is wine glasses clinking. I love drinking champagne. And I love celebrating things with toasts. I used to do that all the time with my beloved Eric. But now I do it with others.

One day, echoes of my aunt's advice swirled around in my head: Go get another degree. I had no intention of getting another degree because I already have a master's. But then I saw an ad for Cornell University's French wines certification. Since wine glasses clinking on my vision board gave me permission, I signed up.

"What will you do with it?" people asked.

"Learn," I replied. I thought I might go work at a winery, but in the end, I just enjoyed learning about domains, appellations, cru, mouthfeel, and then hosting a wine-tasting at my house. As it turned out, I was buried in lectures, tastings, homework, and my final project for three months. It worked wonders distracting me from my desolation.

I am not saying that you should avoid your feelings. You need to feel your feels, but trying something new exercises your mind and gives you confidence. Plus, champagne dulls some of the emotions, but then it also enhances some of the emotions. So, grieving friends, drink a little but not a lot.

My sweet and wonderful Aunt Chu wanted me to go get another degree because she saw that I needed a diversion away from my current post-traumatic death hobby: men.

People love to talk about the women who date a lot and maybe have a little sex after abandonment. They judge it because they have no idea how it feels to lose your identity, to have intimacy ripped away. I met my beloved when I was fourteen. I was never really an individual without him. Ever.

When he died, I didn't know who I was without him. Together, we were the messiest casserole.

Graduating high school together, deciding majors in college

together, never living alone, but straight from our parents' homes to our home. For twenty-eight years, I never decided anything without considering him.

Then suddenly he was gone. I had to learn who I am. What better way to do that than to sit across the dinner table with someone who was interested in me, to take a romantic walk, to hold hands with someone else, to learn to say no… and yes?

Finally, I got tired of my hobby of four dates a week, sometimes three a day. And I realized that I learned who I am, and I now needed to be able to make it through a weekend on my own, while having fun. With myself. Being settled with myself. Knowing a man could not fix my widowhood.

Give yourself permission to try and find yourself in ways other people might feel are unhealthy. They may not know what filling your grief hole feels like. Unhealthy? Who the heck cares? We need to FEEL!

Ball Sports

My late husband was not a sports fan. Politics were his Super Bowl. He had contempt for sports heroes. But today… I am the biggest Chiefs football fan, and I play pickleball twice a week.

"Who are you…?" Eric would say with a funny smirk on his face, no doubt.

Find your passions by trying new things. Ball sports? Church? Bike riding? Volunteering? A new career? Take some time to dream and think, then try some things. You are brave because of what you have gone through. You are the bravest person in the room. Try it!

Seize it! Do it!

Grief Never Ends

I find comfort in that. The other day, almost six years after my husband died, I experienced a huge grief wave while reading a novel. The scene described when the book's star, a paramedic, pulled up to a house where a tiny woman was in the driveway waving her hands like semaphores (signal flags). The shock in her eyes that only someone who is in the process of having her life yanked away can express.

Once, I was that tiny woman, frantically waving the paramedics into my house, expecting them to fix the end of my husband's life and, in many ways, the end of mine. They didn't.

I sat in my chair and sobbed because I knew just how that tiny woman felt. That was me on August 7, 2019. After I had my cry out, I was glad for the sobs. Eric meant that much to me.

I still mourn him. I will always mourn him. This is a privilege that not everyone understands. Grasp that privilege. Swim in it until you are all pruney. As much as you want. Your person is that important.

But then… Move forward.

Reflection

Be patient with yourself. Be so patient with yourself. The biggest part of your heart has just been savagely ripped away. You are in triage.

Time moves forward whether or not you choose to heal. So, invite healing. When the time is right, decide to heal.

Do things.

Be brave.

Have a comeback.

You can choose that.

LISA WOOLERY

After two decades as a public relations executive, Lisa was thrown into widowhood without warning. Not ashamed of her many "hot messes," she shares the challenges of rebuilding life after loss. In *The Widow's Comeback*, she writes with grit, humor, and raw honesty about money, parenting tweens, dating, and faith—offering companionship and hope for the road ahead. She lives in Kansas City with her two teenagers and three rapscallion dogs and loves to travel, play pickleball, and read in her cheetah-print recliner.

CONNECT WITH LISA HERE

www.thewidowscomeback.com

www.empoweredgriefjourney.com/lisa

Scan to learn more about Lisa

20

THE MOMENT OF IMPACT

Geena Hymer

W hen I was eight, Mom packed all of us kids up in the Wagoneer to leave Dad. That day's argument had reached diabolical levels. Unlike any I had ever witnessed from either of them. Dad stood there holding a gun to his head, threatening to end his life right then and there. Mom shouted out at him, "Go ahead and blow your brains out! Let that be the last thing your children see!"

My eyes burn like an inferno from the tears.
What had I just witnessed?
What was that I heard?
There is no way that this is reality.

These emotions boiling over from the kettle in my gut are making me want to vomit, and I feel so very dizzy. Time is at an absolute standstill. A dark villain has arrived and shot this into a freeze-frame Polaroid moment that I don't want to remember.

Although I know that the walls of each and every home from here on out in which I live will be riddled with reminders and flashbacks in frames of wood and gold.

The level of danger revs up and the chatter is now blaring like a bullhorn. My soul feels as though it is being ripped from my tiny body. I am in a fog of disbelief. Surrounded by shouts laced with contempt——demands and ultimatums—I am suffocating in the thick air in this car.

I still wince at the sight of any stupid Wagoneer to this very day. I don't want to lose you, or you, or YOU. My frozen body cries out in my mind. My powerless, innocent childhood eyes should not be seeing this.

How is this going to continue playing out?
How is this going to define my identity and worth as I grow?
Will I overcome the fear of loss?
Will I ever feel as though I am more than enough?
Will this become a new routine—just a normal part of life?

I find myself now cast in the part of instant adult. Suddenly saddled with a daunting, immediate, life-or-death, caregiver role that I did not see coming, let alone know the first thing about navigating. I stumbled through and figured it out.

What was known with certainty was that I believed it necessary to go wherever Dad lived after the dust settled. I felt called to keep him safe. The thought of losing him to a bullet overtakes me. I'm overwhelmed and consumed by a parade of emotions.

One by one, they take their turn in the spotlight, draining any ounce of hope for reconciliation. Leaving me feeling without hope and suddenly deflated.

What had prompted such an extreme reaction?
Were they feeling intense agony, anger, and defeat?

Perhaps it was a moment of desperation amid the thoughts of being without those whom their heart knows best which has caused them to react in the most horrific, irrational of ways.

Dear God, take away this weird sense of shame my delicate eight-year-old self is feeling consumed by. Was I not seen as being valid enough at this moment for them to remain a family unit and for Dad to keep living?

Why is Mom shouting in response to Dad's threat to pull the trigger to go ahead and do it? I find myself challenged to understand my parents' wild reactions and harsh words heard at this time.

The cries and screams from every angle are making my ears feel like they are bleeding. I'm overcome with sorrow and want to throw my body in the middle of the chaos in an effort to make it stop.

I may not have been the eldest, but my older brother was my best friend. I needed him to be by my side at the end of this. He was my "ride or die." My confidant. My seemingly only ally. My little sisters, too small to speak up for themselves, crying in distress from the chaos ensued in this moment from their carseats. They, too, needed saving from the monsters that appear to have overtaken the bodies of our parents.

I honestly do not recollect how the tensions died down that afternoon. What I know is that Mom subsequently drove away with us kids in the Wagoneer where we had been sitting during the unfolding of this traumatic ordeal. We stayed at a family friend's house for support, at least initially.

Nothing got any easier in the next several days that passed. I was anxious with concern about what was next. I was scared of what might happen to my parents in the absence of one another.

Relationships were messy for several years thereafter. I was well into my adulthood before I began making peace with the painful past. No path is fully healed without first ripping open old wounds to then sew them back shut with a seal of complete closure.

My angry parents who had been together for years beyond what they should have been had come to the final breaking point. They had likely loved and respected one another at one point in time, yet were never actually in deep, head over heels love. Due to young, unexpected pregnancy, and the need to make right what was seen as religious wrongdoing, they entered into a marriage that neither one of them essentially wanted or was equipped for.

I have to protect them. My parents. My siblings. I felt incredibly compelled, called upon to step up as this designated, fierce protector of my family from this day forward. To protect them from the harmful acts and damage they are inflicting on every one of us. To make it apparent that I am not going anywhere. Let them know that I am here even if they are unable to be. Plead with them to not create a situation to leave me.

Not like this. Not this day.

Praying they will wait until I am older and can better manage these intense emotions. *Resist the darkness that has a hold of your hands, Dad, let down your guard and drop your arm.*

I'm coming with you, Daddy; I'm coming.

Just don't leave the world like this.

The Courageous Conversation

"If there's anything you want to talk about, I'm here," my dad said many years later. "I'm listening."

Wow! This is it. I have been given the opening that is decades in the making.

Don't back down. Be brave. Be honest. Suck it up and speak now. Shed the skin of fear that has held you captive for as long as you can recall.

It is almost as though he knew without knowing.

I released a deep and labored heave of air from my lungs and my inner child trembled uncontrollably as I began. "Do you remember that afternoon on Bowman Road?"

The day in which, once again, Mom had packed up to leave with us kids. Only this time, it seemed the bag had made it out to the car instead of staying hidden somewhere. I have a memory of once going on a "packed bag hunting mission" to find where the bag had been hidden, only to find it under the kitchen sink where the dishes were being done. I remember grabbing the bag and running.

I continue my conversation with Dad about that ominous day in which our world imploded. A cataclysmic moment of impact that left everything about the future for each and every one of us in question.

While I did not express all the above to Dad, he immediately knew the day to which I referred. The time in the room came to a stand still. My throat started to feel as though it was swelling shut. I held back the urge to cry so I could get out what needed to be said.

I began to share the terror that followed me around daily into every relationship, decision, nightmare, uncomfortable triggering conversation and walked with me into every room, seldom skipping a day ever since. How the moment of witnessing him with a gun to his head as Mom yelled at him has been carried in the marrow of my bones each and every day.

I was still trying to release the everlasting damage that haunted me from the exchange of words between the two of them that day. The screaming and crying. The fear and uncertainty of whether or not any of us would survive that day.

I considered expressing many of my life struggles that followed from this experience, but for whatever reason, I didn't. Even given the opening he provided. I am still protecting us from each other by not always saying everything that needs to be said.

Honest, upfront, and fully transparent communications with those closest to me is still not the easiest of things for me to do in a face-to-face setting. I clam up and I stumble. Weary of other people's reactions.

I do better with writing things down first, so I can be certain to get everything out. All of the hard truths that bring up anxiety and cause a knot to settle in my throat. The terrifying flashbacks that keep my nervous system on the edge of my seat. Moments of deep hidden despair now faded, carried over the years upon the skin. Writing is my love language where I can put my best foot forward with communication.

I've always wanted to share how I fear finding myself trapped in a traumatic, loveless relationship. How I've stumbled through navigating every romantic relationship I have ever had. My inability to maintain a relationship for more than two years or so, due to feeling I lacked the value of being fought for.

How I have been unable to build up the level of trust needed to feel completely safe in the hands of another person…ever. How my inability to communicate my own wants and needs has plagued me at every turn for fear of being rejected.

How I have grieved the loss of every relationship I have had in my life in one form or another. How I grieved the potential loss of Dad—not only on that horrible afternoon but lived in fear daily thereafter for years—not knowing. Simply existing in a state of uncertainty.

How I grieved not being with Mom and my sisters when I moved with him and my brother initially. How I grieved not being with him and my brother when I moved back with Mom and sisters a short time later.

How I have long grieved the early loss of my innocence and how I know I can never retrieve that piece of myself from that day. That a tattered and torn piece of my little soul was carried away in the wind just like the shouts, profanities, and cries—never to be heard from or seen again.

I expressed how uncomfortable I have been around firearms ever since. Whether it was in the holster of a trusted law enforcement officer, on the nightstand for protection by a boyfriend, or hanging up in the back window of an old pickup truck driving down a Montana country road with a knowledgeable good ol' boy going on a hunting trip.

It simply did not matter.

Guns made my skin crawl.

They brought up so many emotions in me.

I did not want to have to explain to anyone the reason behind my discomfort. Alarm bells would go off in my mind, and I would break out in a sweat and my whole body would tense up everywhere.

The above just covers some of the apprehension and trials I faced over the years that stem as a direct result of that terrible day and its aftermath.

I went on to share how responsible I felt for his life after witnessing his intent to die by suicide.

I believe he exhibited deep despair and insecurity about losing his children that day, which was, in my definition, reflected by his decision to take power and control of the situation into his own hands in such an irrational and careless way.

How fearful I was that if he did not have any of us kids with him, he would choose to end his life. That I was responsible for keeping watch over him and being by his side to make sure he remained here on this earth longer and did not abandon us kids in that way. It was a deep-rooted concern and core belief I had until some point into my early adulthood.

As I sat adjacent to my Dad, I could see him digesting the words of my experience from that fateful, long-ago day. After a few thoughtful, silent moments, he began sharing some of his details as well, which aligned with my own.

I released a hefty and freeing internal sigh as he talked. I had put off this conversation for so many years, since I did not know how to approach the topic nor how it would go. I truly believe that this talk was all about the right timing. God's glorious timing.

For the record, I had already had a similar conversation years earlier with my mom. It carried a different level of weight, fears, and feelings attached. With her it was easier to approach and navigate.

When I'd reached the point in our talk in telling Dad how I felt deeply compelled to go with him in the split among the division of assets via the form of children in the divorce and how as a child

I had felt responsible for keeping him alive, our emotions got the better of us.

I stood up and walked over to my dad, embracing him in a long, never-going-to-let-you-go, tight and mighty hug. I knew this moment was guided by the hand of God and absolutely pivotal for us to move towards healing these buried wounds that had kept us covered by dirt and hiding in a tomb of silent and deeply painful scars. It all needed to be dug up and brought into the light in order for each of us to heal after all those years.

The Healing Bang

Now, having had that long-awaited conversation with my dad, I was ready to continue onto the next phase. To grip a gun in my hands, learn to properly operate it, care for it, and shoot it.

Taking back any power, any fear, firearms had over me.

Power in having the ability to defend myself and my family should the need arise.

The love, thought, and intention that went into the gift of a private weapons training class to aid the restoration of self and safety for me is completely priceless. I am forever grateful to my youngest sister for making that happen for me. Closing the loop on the trauma of thirty-eight years earlier. What a blessed way to bring that piece of my story full circle.

As we pulled into the shooting range, I felt my empty stomach begin to churn with nerves. I noticeably was wringing my hands, turning to my sis, letting her know I needed to say a prayer over what was sure to be a highly intense, challenging, yet rewarding experience.

I needed Jesus to lift up my bold heart, to guide my hands and to calm my nerves. After speaking my truth to my Heavenly Father, praying for my instructors and to guide my hands and heal my heart, I was ready to take on the deep meaning behind this imperative day.

"Blessed be the LORD, my rock, who trains my
hands for war, and my fingers for battle."
Psalms 144:1

After watching the videos and signing the contract, we drove over to the shooting site. Stepping out of the car and feeling the gravel under my feet, I knew the moment had come to truly face my fear.

The instructors taught the anatomy of the handgun and the importance of cleaning and proper handling. They then set out several options for me to hold, so I could get an idea of which is best suited for my hand size and grip along with the weight of the guns.

With slight hesitation, I approached the table of laid-out gun choices all staring back at me. If not noticeably with my body language, most definitely I was freaking out in my mind. Yet I forged ahead with the intent of pursuing my goal to defeat fear and overcome my past.

What I believed to be a situation that would make me tremble became a moment of absolute empowerment!

The success of that remarkable day at the shooting range is credited to all the hard work I had done leading up to that forty-sixth trip of mine around the sun. Yes, this is how I spent my birthday.

The tears, conversations, prayers, and therapy sessions had prepared me to take hold of a firearm and aim it at a target with strength in my stature, confidence in my ability, and safety in my surroundings.

By the way, I did INCREDIBLE, and I have the target hanging in my garage to prove it!

I am so very proud of myself for what I accomplished that day. It was no simple feat. I'm grateful for the compassionate instruction I received from my local firearms safety class, which helped me reclaim my power and continue my healing journey.

The Heavenly Nudge

Finding a way out of the chokehold of fear that I was going to lose my entire family that day, grieving the loss of not only my innocence but also the loss of my family as I knew it—placed on us by the darkness of the enemy—I stepped forward bravely wearing the Armor of God, taking back a large part of the power that moment took from me. This is among my greatest victories.

While there is still some healing needed to fully put this beast of mine to rest, I am confident that God's calling for my vulnerability when I was asked to be a part of this anthology was in fact to provide a safe space to heal the final pieces tied to grieving my initial loss of innocence, not only for myself but for others that went through it with me, too.

He called me to share also for those who have walked through similar fires. So that they, too, can see the reflection of another in themselves. Break free from holding tight onto any shame, resentment, pain or responsibility one may harbor when within the grips of darkness and distress.

Today, I release the grief felt from the loss of who I was and what I lived on that awful day.

It does not define me.

It will not control me.

It can no longer hold me back from pursuing and achieving my goals or having successful relationships.

GEENA HYMER

Geena Hymer is fiercely proud of being nineteen years released from the darkness of self-harm and suicidality and ten years into her binge eating disorder recovery. Her life's purpose is helping others find their own path to healing, feeling seen, and having their experiences validated, which is driven by her strong relationship with her Heavenly Father. She's the blessed dog mom to her adopted terrier mix, Bayla. Currently, Geena is working on her first memoir with Hope Books and living with family under the beautiful and often cold blue skies of western Montana.

CONNECT WITH GEENA HERE

https://geenahymer.com
www.empoweredgriefjourney.com/geena

Scan to learn more about Geena

21

AYAHUASCA AND THE SACRED SPIRAL OF GRIEF

Saidi Bess

I trust you, Mother. I trust you, Mother.
I trust you, Mother...

The mantra echoed through my body, mind, and spirit. I realized I had never spoken those words before, never even thought to. The words "trust" and "mother" had never belonged together in my world. I was put up for adoption at birth, severing any inherent sense of trust in a biological mother. And to say I didn't bond well with the woman who adopted me, my new "mother," would be a gross understatement. Trust had no place in that relationship either. But this mother I was surrendering to fully and completely for the first time was Mother Ayahuasca.

I had first read about this sacred plant medicine years earlier, and something deep within me stirred. I knew she would one day be part of my spiritual journey, though I had no idea how. The call was always to meet her at the source—in the jungles of South America—but the idea felt far-off, even impossible. Over time, her presence became more visible in the world, and her call grew louder in my heart. When a dear friend expressed interest in journeying with her, too, everything aligned. I discovered a retreat center in Peru run by respected shamans who had grown up with the medicine. The timing was clear. Within months, I was on my way—uncertain of what would unfold, but trusting it would change me.

In the thick, green jungles of Peru, I found the mother connection I had longed for my entire life. I had come to these sacred lands with the clear intention of healing my deep, unrelenting mother wound. The grief from this loss had shaped so much of my life. This new plant medicine journey was one more modality in my lifelong healing process. Grief has never been linear for me—it spirals, loops, revisits. But each turn brings new awareness. Each pass through the pain feels shorter, gentler, higher in consciousness. This has been the shape of my life: a spiraling grief journey. The early years were the hardest. My mother's absence—her abandonment—left me confused, terrified, ashamed, heartbroken, and hollowed out. I couldn't make sense of it. *Why didn't she want me? What had I done wrong?* Those questions haunted me. And nobody had answers. In those days, people still believed that babies didn't feel. My adoptive mother said I cried constantly, and she didn't understand why. No one did. I didn't even understand it myself. I only knew I was in unbearable pain with no tools, no guidance, no way out.

Until I found drugs and alcohol.

They numbed the pain and gave me a counterfeit version of what I craved: to feel alive, to feel okay in my own skin, to finally feel like I could belong. Of course, that relief was temporary. The substances brought their own version of hell—abusive relationships, homelessness, jails, institutions. Layer upon layer of loss. An epic spiral, downward this time.

Eventually, I found a way out. I've been free from drugs since 1999 and stopped drinking in 2010. Nearly a decade later, in 2019, I began exploring psilocybin as a tool for spiritual growth. The healing and insight I received through that journey deepened my longing to connect with ayahuasca. It felt like the next step—an ancient teacher calling me toward even deeper layers of healing.

For our week of journeying with Mother Ayahuasca, the organizers of the trip asked us to set intentions. Initially when planning this pilgrimage, I thought I was going for other reasons to deepen my spiritual growth, to explore consciousness. But to my surprise, I found myself drawn to working with the grief and wounding around my mother. Again. I felt frustrated that this was still so present, still so dominant, despite all the healing I had already done. But there it was. Once more. We don't get to dictate the timeline of our grief. We just show up for it, remaining open to its pain, its teachings, and its many ways to continue to break our hearts open.

During that first ceremony, the demons came fast and hard. The ceremonies were held at night, in complete darkness, inside a large wooden maloca deep in the jungle. We each lay on individual mats arranged in a circle, with three Peruvian shamans—called maestros—seated at the front. One by one, we approached them to receive the medicine: a small cup of thick, bitter liquid, blessed as they sang *icaros* in Spanish.

These *icaros* are sacred transmissions—the voice of the plant itself. The shamans don't learn them from other people, but directly from the spirit of Ayahuasca through years of deep apprenticeship.

Each chant is a healing transmission, carrying the intelligence of the medicine, guiding us through the journey, opening portals, clearing energy, calling in protection. An authentic ceremony cannot exist without them.

The darkness, the stillness, the deep hum of the jungle just outside—it all created the perfect setting for what was to come. Dark, grotesque images began flooding my psyche. In the past, I feared them. But now I understand: these demons are my fears, visualized...

This night was no different, but something was different. I felt held. Completely held. By this new Mother. This sacred, powerful feminine Presence. "I trust you, Mother," became my anchor as I faced the darkness. I found myself back in the womb—my biological mother's womb. It was a toxic space, heavy with shame, fear, anger, and sorrow. No love. No safety. No welcome. I relived the experience of growing inside that darkness. And then the desperate push through the birth canal, the overwhelming anxiety, the freedom of breaking free from her body... followed immediately by terror. I was alone. I was screaming. I felt the unbearable pull: the desire to be free clashing with a longing to return to the only place I had known, no matter how toxic it was.

I saw the pattern. This was the origin point. My first relationship—dysfunctional and traumatic—set the tone for every other one to follow. The pain, the abandonment, the toxicity: I kept recreating it. This was the grief I carried. Not just from my mother but from how that initial wound kept repeating itself.

Mother Ayahuasca showed me the lineage of pain—the heartbreak—passed down through generations of women in my family, both biological and adopted. I saw how each of them had been affected in their own way. I felt such profound empathy for them and for myself. My heart cracked open under the weight and beauty of that insight. For the first time, I felt mothered.

Held. Understood. Loved.

After experiencing three very different deaths within just a few months, I became fascinated by how uniquely we experience grief and how unequipped our society is to support it. We fear grief. We avoid it. We deny our mortality. That realization shifted everything for me.

I devoted myself to formal studies in death, dying, and bereavement, earning an associate's degree in gerontology, a bachelor's in social work, and ultimately a master's degree in thanatology—the specialized study of death, dying, and grief. Thanatology goes beyond theory; it equips professionals across fields—healthcare workers, counselors, chaplains, hospice staff, funeral directors, and others—to support people navigating the complex emotions, spiritual upheaval, and transitions surrounding death.

This academic path gave me both the language and the framework to understand my own lifelong grief journey. Everything clicked. I became aware that I had been living a lifelong grief journey, and I hadn't even known it. The loss of my mother at birth wasn't seen as a "real" loss. It was invisible. Unacknowledged. But it has shaped every corner of my life.

I began to understand terms like disenfranchised grief, ambiguous loss, and post-traumatic growth, and each one spoke directly to my story. My grief had never been validated, but here was the language and the framework that finally made sense of it all. It wasn't just my experience. I started seeing that many of us are carrying unrecognized grief from breakups, estranged relationships, health changes, identity shifts, and childhood wounds. Loss that never gets named and therefore never gets supported. My spiritual path deepened. I was introduced to the concept of ancestors. At first, I couldn't relate. Having been adopted and knowing nothing about my biological lineage, I felt rootless, almost like I came from nowhere. Others spoke of ancestors and lineage with reverence. I felt... nothing.

But that began to change. I was taught that healing our ancestral lines is one of the most powerful things we can do—not just for them, but also for ourselves. That the energy they carried—the unprocessed pain, grief, shame, and trauma—still lived on in us. That time and space are human constructs. That our ancestors are not in the past—they're right here with us, energetically present. And that healing can happen across dimensions. This made sense to me in a way I couldn't explain. So I followed the teachings. I built an ancestor altar. I began to speak to them. I sent them love. I acknowledged the pain they carried. I told them I trusted their decisions. I expressed my own grief. And something opened. I started receiving messages. Intuitive knowing. The energy began to shift. Their healing became my healing. As they released what they'd been carrying, I began to release what I had inherited. It changed everything—my body, my mind, and my spirit. For the first time in my life, I felt connected. I had a lineage. I had roots. I was not alone.

After connecting with my biological lineage, I turned my attention to my adoptive family. I began the same process—offering love, compassion, and healing energy to the pain they, too, had carried. The messages that came through were filled with gratitude, softness, and support. That relationship deepened in ways I never imagined possible. I saw the pain in their lineage, too—the grief that shaped their choices, the patterns they inherited. It was never personal. It was generational.

I came to understand, in a profound way, that everyone—my mothers, my grandmothers, my father—was simply carrying what had been passed to them. Pain moves through families until someone is ready to feel it, face it, and transmute it. That someone became me. And as I embraced this healing work, I began to feel my own pain shift. The blaming, the bitterness, the sense of abandonment—I let it all go. I released the grip of victim-consciousness that had shaped the first half of my life. I used to believe the world was out to get me. That I was cursed. That life was suffering, and I needed to defend myself against it. But that was never the truth. I now understand that we are all doing the best we can with the cards we're dealt. Most of us don't mean to hurt others. We act from our wounds. From unconsciousness. From our own unresolved grief.

Ancestral healing changed me. It gave me context, compassion, and clarity. It helped me reclaim my power and remember who I am, not just a wounded child, but a soul with agency, purpose, and deep wisdom. This is the power of grief work. It's not just about sorrow; it's about freedom, too. When we heal our grief, we begin to heal the collective. We interrupt the pattern. We become the alchemists.

We are living in a very different time now. We have tools our ancestors never had. Breathwork. Plant medicine. Energy healing. Therapy. Spiritual community. These resources weren't available to the generations before us—they didn't have the language or the support to move through their pain. But we do. And with those tools comes a responsibility not to judge the past but to transform the future.

This is sacred work. It's the work of soul remembrance. It's not about blaming, bypassing, or fixing. It's about honoring what has been, loving what is, and choosing a new way forward. It's vital that we understand the sacred role of loss on the spiritual path. Grief is not something to "get over." It's not something broken that needs fixing. It is a powerful initiator. It cracks us open to truths we may never have otherwise touched. Yes, it can bring deep sorrow, confusion, and despair—but it can also be the doorway to awakening, transformation, and boundless love.

Loss expands us—if we let it. So many of us get stuck in our pain. We harden. We isolate. We use grief as a reason to check out from life. But when we allow it to soften us instead—when we let ourselves feel, grieve, honor, and learn—we begin to experience the deeper invitation: to love in a bigger way. To love beyond a person. Beyond form. Beyond time and space. I now understand that my mother's departure at birth wasn't just a tragedy—it was also a portal. One that cracked open my capacity to love more deeply than I ever thought possible. It was not a punishment—it was a path. A soul agreement. A gift in disguise.

Books like Michael Newton's *Journey of Souls* helped me make sense of this—how we choose, before incarnation, the experiences and relationships that will best support our soul's evolution. That we don't "lose" people at all. We collaborate. We learn through contrast. We love each other enough to play the hard roles. The ones we lose love us so much as to give us this profound gift, this amazing opportunity to love even bigger.

This isn't about spiritual bypassing. I've felt every ounce of the pain. I've screamed, sobbed, collapsed under the weight of it. But I've also risen. With every spiral, I've found new meaning. With every loss, a deeper truth has emerged.

That truth is this:

There is no real loss.
There is only transformation.

There is only more love.

We're being called now, as a collective, to reclaim grief as a sacred teacher—not just something to survive, but something to learn from. Whether the loss is a death, a relationship, a dream, a home, or a version of self…the wound holds wisdom. So ask yourself:

What is this loss here to teach me?
How is it shaping who I'm becoming?
Where is it opening my heart?
What deeper connection is possible now?

Let grief guide you—not just back into your sorrow but forward into your soul.

I now feel held by something much larger than I ever imagined. A Cosmic Mother. A universal, all-encompassing love. I believe we all have access to this when we turn inward, when we trust our journey, when we allow the pain to become our teacher.

Grief is not the end of the story.

It is the sacred threshold.

And what lies beyond it… is love.

SAIDI BESS

Saidi Bess is a sacred sexuality guide, energy healer, and the founder of Sacred Sensual Alchemy. With a master's degree in thanatology and a deep devotion to spiritual healing, she brings a unique understanding of grief—especially non-death related loss—into all aspects of her work. Saidi weaves energy work, sacred sexuality, and pilgrimage to sacred sites into powerful pathways for healing and transformation. She contributed a chapter to a collaborative book called *Beyond Certainty: Finding Courage to Embrace the Unknown.*

CONNECT WITH SAIDI HERE

www.sacredsensualalchemy.com
www.empoweredgriefjourney.com/saidi

Scan to learn more about Saidi

22

GRIEF IN MOTHERHOOD

Kaitlin Parsons

My husband Jordan and I had two beautiful little boys, and we decided to grow our family again in 2021. We were excited, and even more so when we found out we were having our first daughter. I had a healthy pregnancy and yet, at our twenty-week scan, we heard those terrible words no parent wants to ever hear—our baby girl no longer had a heartbeat. The next day, my doctor induced labor, and I delivered Esme Ruth. We got to hold her tiny body and say goodbye to her.

When we conceived again, I was cautious but hopeful. But unfortunately, at thirteen weeks into the pregnancy, during another scan, we heard those dreaded words, "I'm sorry there's no heartbeat" again. A few days later, our baby girl was born on May 10th, and we named her Adelaide Hope.

After losing two babies, I wasn't sure I could try again. But something in me needed to keep hoping. My husband and I went through test after test with no real answers as to why we lost the girls. I was deemed healthy and given the go-ahead to try again.

After months of prayers, tears, and heartache, we decided to give it one more try. We were very cautiously optimistic, hopeful yet scared to death. We made it through every milestone, but two weeks before her due date, the morning of my thirty-seven-week appointment, I knew something was wrong. When I woke up, I did not feel the baby move like she always did. When I got to the doctor's office, I knew before they even had to tell me. They sent me to the hospital right away, and about twelve hours later, we met our precious baby girl, Lainey Grace. She was full-term and showed no signs of any issues. I can still tell you exactly how she felt, how she smelled, the outline of her lips. She was perfect, and yet she was silent.

Just hours before delivery, she'd been moving inside me, still alive. When she was born, she was beautiful. Her pale skin and her lips were just like her big brothers'. We kissed her over and over. I can still remember the feeling of her warm little body resting on my chest. And my heart broke again. I kept hoping I'd wake up from the nightmare. But I didn't. Because this really was goodbye. Again. Just like it had been for her sisters, two years earlier.

Grief consumed me. I was physically exhausted, emotionally raw, spiritually questioning. When you lose one child, your identity shifts. When you lose three, it shatters. I will be completely honest—I wrestled with my faith in God. I screamed. I doubted. But I also found pieces of grace in the silence.

They say grief is just love with nowhere to go and nothing left to hold.

Numbness.

Sadness.

Anger.

And then comes desperate hope.

Hope that it isn't real.

That, somehow, this isn't happening.

How could this happen to me?

How could this happen again?

There's no way to comprehend saying goodbye to your baby, the baby you were supposed to meet in two short weeks. The baby you made plans for, especially after already saying goodbye to two precious babies before her.

Then reality sets in.

I still have a husband and two living boys who need their mama.

They need love, care, and presence.

But how do I show up when I'm shattered?

They're grieving, too. They also lost their sister.

So how do we move forward? How do we live with this ache? Grief didn't just happen to me, it happened to all of us. And learning how to carry it together was part of the journey.

The one thing I continued to ask was *why?* A few months after we lost Lainey Grace, further testing by a specialist determined that I lost my girls due to small placentas. This I didn't know until it was too late, which is why I now advocate for measuring placental health during pregnancy.

My boys have continued to heal me. Especially my rainbow baby boy, August, who was born a year after we lost Lainey. He came after the storm, bringing light when we needed it most.

Now it has been two years without our Lainey Grace.

Two years of carrying both grief and joy.

Two years since we said our quiet hello and heartbreaking goodbye on August 1, 2023.

Honestly, the only thing I have ever wanted was to become a mother, so when I did, I found the greatest love I have ever known. I always thought I understood love. Then I became a mother and it deepened. Then I became a grieving mother and it changed me forever. The way I lived and loved and even mothered my earthly boys.

People often ask how I keep going. The truth is, I don't always know. But I do know this: Grief stripped me bare, but what remained was love—intentional, patient, present. Now, I'm a mom of three beautiful boys who fill my days with noise, laughter, and purpose.

I'm also the mother of three baby girls—Esme Ruth, Adelaide Hope, and Lainey Grace, who live in my heart and in heaven. My daughters taught me that time doesn't determine motherhood—love does. They didn't get the chance to grow up here on Earth, but they changed everything for me. My daughters gave me a reason to keep living because they gave me a purpose that rose from my pain. Through them, something else was born: a mission to help other grieving mothers feel seen, heard, and held. They are why I write this, and why I speak publicly. I began my podcast, *Grief in Motherhood*, to create the space I so desperately needed—the kind of space where it's okay to cry, to question, to rage, and still be a mother. A space where we don't have to pretend to be "okay," and where our babies' names are spoken with reverence, not avoided in discomfort.

This podcast isn't just storytelling. It's a sacred connection. It's survival. It's healing in motion. It's the place where our pain is honored, our motherhood is validated, and our love is never questioned even when the world forgets our babies were real. Through each episode, I get to walk with other loss moms through the darkness, sometimes offering light, sometimes simply sitting with them. And in doing so, I'm reminded that even in grief, there can be growth. Even in heartbreak, there can be meaning. And even in silence, there is a tribe of loss moms who carry so much grief and love.

I've learned that our stories matter. Speaking our babies' names matters. Giving ourselves permission to grieve fully and honestly is one of the greatest gifts we can offer ourselves and each other.

I honor Esme, Adelaide, and Lainey in simple, sacred ways, having cake and lighting candles on their birthdays, saying their names, writing their initials in the sand, and talking to them when I'm alone. I see them in the eyes of the women who message me after listening to an episode of my podcast to say, "I thought I was alone," or "Thank you for sharing your story."

To other grieving parents:

If you are holding grief in your body, your heart, your womb—know that you are not alone. Your pain is valid. Your love is eternal. And your baby matters. You don't have to rush your healing. You don't have to hide your tears. You don't have to fit anyone's timeline.

This chapter is for the daughters who made me a mother; for the sons who made me keep living; for the women who are finding their way through the ache. We are not alone in this. There's no map for this journey. But there are fellow travelers. And we will walk it together.

I wish this wasn't my story. I wish I could write about lullabies and baby milestones. I wish I could describe Esme's laugh, Adelaide's first steps, or Lainey's sleepy snuggles. But I can't. What I can do is keep saying their names. Keep honoring their lives. Keep telling the truth about baby loss—even when it's uncomfortable. Because silence doesn't protect us. It isolates us. And I believe our babies deserve more than silence. They deserve legacy. They deserve love that's spoken out loud.

KAITLIN PARSONS

Kaitlin is a wife and mother navigating the delicate balance of parenting her three boys on Earth while grieving the loss of her three daughters. Through her grief coaching and *Grief in Motherhood* podcast, Kaitlin provides a community for mothers who have experienced loss, ensuring they can find connection, support, and understanding. With an open heart and firsthand experience of navigating motherhood after loss, Kaitlin is dedicated to walking alongside other moms, offering light, hope, and the reminder that even in grief, they are not alone.

CONNECT WITH KAITLIN HERE

https://linktr.ee/Kaitlinparsons6
www.empoweredgriefjourney.com/kaitlin

Scan to learn more about Kaitlin

23

WHERE HER HANDS ONCE WERE

Jill McClennen

I vividly remember walking out the back door of my grandmother's kitchen for the last time a few years after she died, stepping out onto the back steps into the warm July sunshine, leaving a part of my life behind that shaped me into who I am today.

My grandmother died in 2011 after ninety-four years of life, after living in that house for over seventy years, and I was walking away from the home I grew up in. Grandmom grew up on a farm in the southern part of New Jersey. When she got engaged to my grandfather, he purchased land in the city close by to build her a modest home with a backyard for her to plant a garden, which was one of the things she wanted most. It was not a big city like Philadelphia, where some of her sisters moved after marrying, but it was a city compared to the farm. This was the house that I ended up being raised in, spending many days and nights exploring every nook and cranny of the house from the basement to the attic.

Many women who raise children alone often lean on their family for support. Their mothers, fathers, and siblings fill the void left by the missing parent—in our case, my dad, who wasn't around. My grandmother, my mother's mother, stepped in and took on the role of caring for me as a child. She was the person I would turn to when I needed advice, teaching me about life and what is important to thrive and feel good about myself.

The more I think about the past, especially my childhood and early adult years, the more I realize that she was so much more than a grandmother to me. In my life, she played many roles, and I am so thankful to have had her. Not only was she the typical grandma, she also played the role of parent, since my father wasn't around much and my mother worked a lot. She was also my friend. I enjoyed talking with her even when we disagreed about things. If there was ever something I didn't know, I would ask her before anyone else. If she didn't know, then we would ask someone else or look it up together, but especially when it came to sewing, cooking, housekeeping, gardening, house plants; she was the expert as far as I am concerned. I wish we could still make new memories together and that she could help me on my journey of being a mom, but it's okay. Sometimes I think I know what she would be telling me to do, even though she isn't here to tell me.

For almost five years, my husband and I lived with Grandmom in that house my grandfather built for her, and we helped care for her—especially during her last few months when she needed support twenty-four hours a day. We moved into the attic of her house, which she had lovingly converted into a bedroom for us. That space carried so many memories; as a child, I had spent countless afternoons there, trying on my mother's old prom and bridesmaid dresses from the 60's, putting on old wigs and shoes that were too big for me, and flipping through old books pretending I was a grown-up working woman.

Before moving back home, I had been living in San Francisco, clear across the country from both my mother and grandmother. I carried the fear that my grandmother might die while I was gone, and that I'd never see her again. During those years, I got married, and my husband and I dreamed of opening a bakery. When she suggested we return to New Jersey, live with her, and help keep her in her home while we built our business without the burden of rent, it felt like the right decision.

Even so, I was anxious. I had left New Jersey swearing I'd never come back, and I worried what it would feel like to return, surrounded by people who remembered an earlier version of me. Yet I've never regretted it. Sharing the last years of her life was a gift—her death has deeply affected me and put me on a new path I would have never dreamed of.

My best memories from the last year of Grandmom's life were the nights I sat in her room talking with her while I was pregnant with my first child. I would come home from working in the bakery and sit on her bed, and she would be in her chair rocking gently. We would talk about everything. Our hopes and our fears for my unborn child, and the fact that neither of us ever thought we would see this day. In her bedroom was a vanity with a large round mirror that had been there since before I was born. From where I sat, I could see myself reflected in the glass, my belly growing a little more each week. She and I watched it grow together, sharing both the wonder of new life and the tender awareness that her life was drawing to a close.

In those years, an ordinary day with her held both familiarity and change. At first, she was fully able to care for herself, but slowly I began to notice signs that she needed more help. She had always been independent, insisting on washing her clothes in the basement and carrying them outside to hang on the line, even in the middle of winter when they seemed like they would freeze solid. She took great pride in her home, cooking meals, keeping things tidy, and every year, washing and hanging her curtains in the spring and fall to mark the change in seasons. These rhythms had been part of her life for decades, and it was hard for her to let them go. It became a struggle between us, sometimes a full-on fight, as I learned to step in more, and she learned to allow me to.

Even as her independence shifted, some rituals remained steady and grounding for us both. Our nightly chats became a thread weaving through the last years of her life. I wish now that I had recorded them, writing down the details of her stories and the wisdom she offered. Late at night, after our conversations ended, she would sit alone in her darkened room and pray the rosary with the glow-in-the-dark beads that had belonged to her mother. From the living room, I could hear the gentle squeak of her chair rocking back and forth as she prayed. That sound, soft and steady in the night, was as comforting to me as her presence. It reminded me that even as things were changing, some pieces of her life and faith endured until the end.

For the last few weeks of her life, she was in hospice care, and during that time, she changed so much that I was already grieving—because, in many ways, she was already gone. In the last few years, especially the last few months, we argued like we never had before. There was one night after I had struggled getting her to settle down that I told my husband that maybe God was doing this so I wouldn't miss her as much when she was gone.

Seeing my grandmother in her bedroom, but now in a hospital bed by the window, was a shift that brought me closer to the realization that she was dying. Bringing hospice on board was such a help for our whole family. When the nurses were there, I found myself asking a lot of questions, and their answers helped me feel more at ease and approach the situation differently. I learned that so much of what was happening was normal and natural for a body at the end of life.

Grandmom started talking in her sleep and reaching out her arm, like she was trying to grab someone's hand. Sometimes she'd say out loud that she couldn't reach it or that they were too far away. It was strange and kind of creepy, like someone invisible was there. I couldn't help but find it fascinating, especially after learning this happens to people at the end of their lives.

When she had moments of clarity, I was able to talk to her and ask questions, to have conversations that hopefully gave her some closure. We had a series of honest, emotional conversations about family tensions, her worries for me and my family, and even my difficult relationship with my dad.

A few times during our conversations, she closed her eyes, and I thought she was asleep. Then she'd say something that made complete sense, so I kept talking. Sometimes talking to her out loud was more for me, rather than trying to communicate anything to her. It felt better to have something to do while sitting with her, speaking my thoughts out loud rather than sitting and watching her fade away. I now know that hearing is one of the last things that a person loses at the end of life. Listening to a loved one talk can be very comforting for a person—hearing their voice even if what they are saying is not important. I find a lot of comfort in the thought of her hearing my voice as she drifted towards death, just as I would hear her voice as a child when she would tell me bedtime stories about her growing up on a farm and I would feel so relaxed and comfortable that I could drift off to sleep.

On the day she died, I had already felt that she was not with us anymore. She was no longer talking or opening her eyes, her breathing changed, and it felt different to be with her. There was a lack of life with her—the body was on autopilot and doing what it needed to do, but she was not there. I wanted to be there the moment she died, but she had other plans. A few hours after I left her hospice bedside, I got the call that she was gone.

The next morning, it felt so strange to be in her house, knowing there was no more Grandmom. I woke up after spending the evening sitting on the porch crying after I got the phone call from my mom telling me she was gone. I remember thinking how amazing it is that life can change so drastically in an instant, yet it still goes on. The neighborhood dogs are still barking, my son who was six months old at that time still woke up in the morning smiling and needing attention. Life still goes on all around us after someone we love dies. We all live and die, and that's the way it's supposed to be. But that first morning really sucked; my eyes and head and heart hurt.

Getting ready for the viewing and funeral, I went through old photos to display, and that helped me feel that she was still with me. Seeing a younger version of Grandmom smiling and dancing started to replace some of the harder images from her final weeks. It wasn't all bad—kissing her forehead, talking with her in those moments of clarity, and telling her I loved her was special, but the woman in those photos was the one I wanted to remember.

After getting dressed for the viewing, I went to Grandmom's room and used her mirror, the large round vanity mirror that I had used my entire life to see my full outfit, even when I was a child playing dress-up. The hard part was that I couldn't ask Grandmom, "So how do I look?" like I usually did after checking myself out. Tonight, I couldn't do that because I was getting dressed to go to her viewing, and it hit me that she was really gone. It was starting to set in: Grandmom is gone and won't be coming back. Logically, I knew this, but in that moment my heart felt it deeply. It went beyond tears; it was a deep ache in my chest that I knew only time would heal.

In the weeks that followed, I spent time sorting through her things. Letting go of her belongings was one of the hardest things for me to do. I knew it had to be done, but I felt guilty, like she might come home and wonder where her clothes had gone. After so many years in that house, everything had its place—tables that hadn't been moved in twenty or thirty years. Removing anything felt like losing another piece of her.

Taking care of her those last few years of her life and especially the last few weeks of her life helped my grieving process. It allowed me to spend time with her, have conversations with her that I cherished, and let her go little by little, starting the grieving process and caring for her as she cared for me when I was a child. It helped me to feel my grief in a way that was not overwhelming. This process of letting go over time, being there to experience her dying over a few years—but even more so in those last few weeks—nourished my soul in a way that helped to move me through the grieving process even before she died. I never got to the point that I felt as if it would swallow me whole, so I could allow myself to feel the grief fully instead of fighting it.

After she died, my husband, my son, and I stayed in her house for three more years before we moved and left it behind. A few weeks after she died, one night, while reheating food and opening the oven to grab one of her cast iron pans, the pain of missing her hit me like a ton of bricks. I felt sick to my stomach, sat on the old linoleum floor, leaned back against the oven door, and cried. It's wonderful that I was able to live in her house with my family, but everywhere I turned, there were reminders of her, especially in her kitchen where I spent so much of my childhood learning how to cook with her.

Over the years, I've learned that if we resist feeling grief—if we spend a lot of energy trying to pretend we are not feeling what we are feeling—then grief can destroy us. The alternative is to allow yourself to feel it fully, to transform yourself, like a phoenix rising from the ashes. You are not who you were before your loss, and that's okay. Who comes out the other end is a new person.

Walking away from who we were means that person doesn't exist anymore; it means stepping into who we are now.

Grief shows up in our bodies as much as in our minds and hearts. Every thought and emotion leaves a physical imprint. Sometimes we feel exhausted, we ache, or we experience a weight on our chest without realizing what we carry until we start to move.

One of the most powerful ways to care for yourself during grief is movement—not pushing through workouts, but tuning in to what your body needs. Movement can be walking, stretching, or swaying to music. Let your body tell you what it needs. On some days, you may want to dance wildly; on others, you may simply want to lie down and breathe with your hands on your heart.

Moving your body helps bring you back to the present, giving your mind a break from looping pain or anxiety. Move the part of your body where you feel grief most. Maybe it's in your chest, your gut, or your throat. Make sounds if needed; humming, sighing, or deep exhaling can release stuck energy. Let your heart lead. This isn't about doing it "right" but listening, respecting, and moving with what's true for you. Grief will transform, little by little, when the body leads.

In the years since Grandmom died, my life has changed in so many ways. My experience with her at the end of her life inspired me to begin working in the end-of-life and grief space. It showed me all the ways I was unprepared and uneducated about the realities of end-of-life. And that I could help others be better prepared for all of it.

The bad parts of navigating the end of life with someone will fade with time. Eventually, you'll remember your loved one as they were at their best.

My grandmother would be proud of my life, especially my parenting and relationship with my mother, which she always worried about. I adore my life and feel surrounded by so much love and support. I know Grandmom would've enjoyed watching my children grow and seeing the career I built, but she would've struggled with the chaos and clutter that comes with small children. As much as I miss her, I realize that it was time for her to move on to another world and for children to move into ours.

Moving forward doesn't mean forgetting. It means carrying love forward differently. Grief strips us bare but also shows us who we are and helps us discover who we want to be moving forward. Even when you still miss someone, you can keep growing.

If I could whisper something in your ear, like a little fairy visiting, I would say the more you fight grief the longer it lasts and the harder it is to move forward. But you don't have to do this work alone. Find the support you need, such as a counselor or grief guide. Use tools like journaling to process your emotions, and be sure to incorporate some movement into each day.

Grief is natural and an unavoidable part of living life in this human form. It's a reflection of love and connection with others, and when that connection is broken by death or a relationship ending, we feel that loss in our bodies. When you allow yourself to fully feel grief—sadness, anger, confusion, and even moments of peace—you give yourself a chance to process it instead of carrying it unspoken.

Grief can open us up. When we don't run from it, it deepens our appreciation for life, strengthens relationships, and helps us live with more presence and purpose.

JILL MCCLENNEN

Jill McClennen is a certified death doula, yoga instructor, host of the *Seeing Death Clearly* podcast, and designer of death-positive apparel. Her journey into this work began when she cared for her grandmother at the end of her life, and now Jill helps others navigate death anxiety, end-of-life preparation, illness, caregiving, dying, and grief.

CONNECT WITH JILL HERE

www.endoflifeclarity.com
www.empoweredgriefjourney.com/jill

Scan to learn more about Jill

CLOSING REFLECTION

Your Empowered Grief Journey Begins Here

You have just walked through twenty-three stories of grief, loss, courage, and rebirth. Each one was written by someone who dared to face their pain and transform it into something meaningful. These stories are proof of resilience, vulnerability, and hope. It is in their truth that we can see our own reflection. In their courage, we can find the strength to keep going. It is through their healing that we are reminded that transformation is possible for every one of us. Grief is not a solitary path but a shared human experience.

The Empowered Grief Journey™ was born from the heartbreaking loss of my son, Caden. His brief but powerful life became the spark that lit this vision. What began as my search for meaning evolved into a movement of voices, each rising from the ashes of their own pain to stand in the light of healing. Together, we've created something bigger than our individual stories: a collective testament to the power of love, remembrance, and renewal. This living legacy will continue to inspire healing for generations to come.

Empowered grief is not about "moving on." It's about moving through. We are being asked to walk beside our pain, to listen to it, and to let it shape us in new ways. Healing doesn't erase our loss; it transforms it. It's the process of learning how to carry our grief differently, to turn pain into purpose and remembrance into light.

To you, the reader, thank you for walking this path with us. Thank you for allowing yourself to feel, reflect, and hope as you turned these pages. Whether your loss is fresh or decades old, whether you're standing in the rubble or rising from it, know this: you are not alone. Your story matters. Your healing matters.

As you close this book, may you continue to discover your own empowered grief journey and carry forward the wisdom shared in these pages. Grief is an evolution. It changes us, softens us, and teaches us to see the hidden gifts, lessons, and blessings that await within the brokenness of loss. Continue your journey with courage and grace as you heal at your own pace.

From grief, we learn compassion. From pain, we discover purpose. And from loss, we learn how to love in deeper ways than we ever thought possible. This is the alchemy of healing, the transformation of suffering into strength, isolation into connection, and endings into new beginnings.

May Caden's light, and the light of every soul remembered in these pages, remind us that even in our darkest moments, love never disappears; it only changes form, guiding us ever forward. Together, we carry the light forward, turning loss into legacy

ACKNOWLEDGMENTS

To the incredible authors who poured their hearts into these pages: Thank you for your courage, honesty, and unwavering vulnerability. You have turned your deepest pain into purpose and given a voice to what so many feel but cannot say. Your willingness to stand in your truth and transform grief into healing has created a ripple of hope that will touch countless lives. Together, we have shown that even in the darkest moments, light can emerge, and in that light, we've built something greater than ourselves: a movement of healing, courage, and love.

Thank you to the team behind these pages:

Teresa Syms — My heartfelt gratitude to you for writing such a powerful and compassionate foreword. Your words beautifully set the tone for this book and capture the spirit of what The Empowered Grief Journey™ stands for—turning pain into purpose, creating light from loss, and reminding us that grief, when embraced with love, becomes a source of profound transformation.

Alice Douthwaite of Paper-Free Editing — You challenged us to tell our stories with clarity and power. Your guidance was kind, supportive, and thorough. You generously shared thoughtful questions and precise suggestions that brought our chapters to life, adding emotional depth that will resonate with readers. At every step, you offered steady encouragement and showed deep care and empathy for this project.

Kristina Mamone — My best friend and wife. You have walked beside me along every step of this journey, reminding me each day that even in grief, we can continue to build a life with meaning and love. You took on the challenge of designing and creating a beautiful book cover and compiling the chapters to make this anthology a memorable piece that honors grief in a new light.

To the Empowered Grief Community

From contributors, podcast listeners and guests, to early readers, and those who showed up to share your reflections, your feedback helped us create a one of a kind unique perspective on grief that will support people of all beliefs and backgrounds in communities across the world.

To Friends and Family

Thank you for the love, patience, and behind-the-scenes support that made this project possible. Your willingness to open the door to hard, but healing conversations gave us courage. As we wrote, many of you shared that these pages stirred long-buried grief and invited long-delayed healing. Hearing this renewed our faith in the work and reminded us that the purpose of this anthology is larger than any one voice. Thank you for giving us a glimpse of its impact and reach. What comes next is bigger than we could have imagined.

To Our Readers

Thank you for your courage. Grief asks us to face the depths of our pain and carry forward with strength and compassion. By choosing to walk this path, you've already begun transforming your loss into empowerment. Allow these stories to remind you of the power that lives within you. The power to rise, to rebuild, and to reclaim your light from the ashes of loss. You are never alone on this journey, and together we can navigate grief with courage and compassion.

With gratitude,

Chris Mamone

CONTINUE YOUR EMPOWERED GRIEF JOURNEY

You've walked through stories of
courage, acceptance, and healing.
But your journey doesn't end here.

This is your invitation to keep growing, connecting,
and discovering the empowered version of you
that grief has been guiding you toward.

JOIN THE EMPOWERED GRIEF COLLECTIVE

A private Facebook community where hearts healing
through loss come together for weekly reflections,
live discussions, and mutual support.

JOIN HERE

www.facebook.com/groups/empoweredgriefcollective

RECEIVE MONTHLY INSPIRATION

Sign up for *The Empowered Grief Journey* newsletter.
Sent once a month with reflections, journal prompts, and
guided encouragement to help you move
from pain to empowerment.

SUBSCRIBE HERE

EmpoweredGriefJourney.com/newsletter

READY TO TAKE YOUR HEALING DEEPER?

WORK WITH CHRIS

Chris offers compassionate grief coaching,
grounded in the **CADEN Framework**

*Courage, Acceptance, Deep Healing,
Empowerment, and New Beginnings.*

FREE EMPOWERED GRIEF CALL

Book a complimentary session to explore where you
are on your journey and what support could help you
move forward with confidence and clarity.

SCHEDULE YOUR FREE CALL HERE

EmpoweredGriefJourney.com/call

ONE-ON-ONE AND GROUP COACHING

Through personalized coaching sessions, Chris helps
you uncover meaning in your grief, cultivate
self-acceptance, and realign with your authentic
purpose—one courageous step at a time.

LEARN MORE HERE

EmpoweredGriefJourney.com/coaching

STAY CONNECTED WITH THE EMPOWERED GRIEF JOURNEY PODCAST

Listen to stories of transformation, healing, and
hope from guests who have turned loss into legacy.

Follow on **Apple Podcasts**, **YouTube**,
and your favorite platforms.

LEARN MORE HERE

EmpoweredGriefJourney.com/podcast

You are not alone. Your story matters.
And your empowered grief journey is only just beginning.

SCAN THE QR CODE BELOW
TO LEARN MORE

NOTES

NOTES

www.ingramcontent.com/pod-product-compliance
Lightning Source LLC
Chambersburg PA
CBHW071631140626
46555CB00022B/2054